OBJECTIVE TYPE QUESTIONS FOR LIBRARY AND INFORMATION SCIENCE

(Tabulation Analysis format for Competitive Examinations)

OBJECTIVE TYPE QUESTIONS FOR LIBRARY AND INFORMATION SCIENCE

(Tabulation Analysis Format for Competitive Examinations)

By

DR. SURESH KUMAR KAGRA

M. Lib. & Inf. Sc, (UGC-NET), M. Phil, Ph.D. (LIS)

Kurukshetra University, Kurukshetra-136119

Ess Ess Publications

New Delhi

OBJECTIVE TYPE QUESTIONS FOR LIBRARY AND INFORMATION SCIENCE
(Tabulation Analysis format for Competitive Examinations)

ISBN: 978-93-87698-79-6
Price : Rs. 775/-

First Published 2021

Published by:
Ess Ess Publications
4831/24, Ansari Road,
Darya Ganj,
New Delhi-110 002.
INDIA
Phones: 23260807, 41563444
Fax: 41563334
E-mail: info@essessreference.com
www.essessreference.com

Cover Design by *Patch Creative Unit*

Printed and bound in India

Dedicated to
My father **Mr. JAGDISH**
and
Mother **Smt. SANTOSH DEVI**

Contents

Preface

There has been an exponential growth in number of colleges and universities imparting library education in recent past which has also led to an equal growth in number of students opting for this career. Post Masters' one can quickly get employment opportunities in this profession but for that everyone who wishes to get employed has to clear either State level or National level eligibility examination which often does not prove to be a cake-walk.

This book is written with the objective to impart knowledge and skills to the aspirants so that they may clear the aforementioned examination without much difficulty. The book has been carefully divided into sections and language has been kept lucid so as to enable those from non-English background also to grasp the subject matter without much difficulty. This text could be called first of its kind because this book does not only have questions and their answers but also information pertaining to the profession in multiple choice format. An attempt has been made to get the aspirant the very gist of the subject being discussed without beating about the bush.

I shall welcome all constructive suggestions from the readers and would try to incorporate them in subsequent editions.

— Suresh Kumar Kagra

1

Library and Information Society

DR. S.R. RANGNATHAN (1892-1972) LIBRARY BOOKS PUBLICATIONS

S. N.	Books	Years	Publishers / Places
1	Five Laws of Library Science	1931	MLA/ Edward Goldstone, London
	Colon Classification	1933	Madras Univ. Library and MLA
2	Classified Catalogue Code	1934	MLA /G. Blunt & Sons, London
	Library Administration	1935	Asia Publishing House, Bombay
3	Prolegomena to Library Classification	1937	MLA/ Edward Goldstone, London
4	Theory of The Library Catalogue	1938	Madras library Assoc., Madras
5	Elements of Library Classification	1945	Asia Publishing House, Bombay
6	Classification and international Documentation	1948	Asia Publishing House, Bombay
7	Classification and Communication	1951	University of Delhi, Delhi
8	Documentation Genesis and Development	1951	Vikas Publishing House, Delhi
9	Manual of Library Classification	1951	ILA, Ashoka Pub, Delhi
10	Philosophy of Library Classification	1951	Univ. of Minnesota, U.S.

11	Headings and Canons	1955	S. Viswanathan, Madras
12	Reference Service	1961	Asia Publishing House, Bombay
13	Documentation and its facts	1963	Asia Publishing House, Bombay
14	Descriptive Account of Colon Classification	1965	Asia Publishing House, Bombay
15	Library Book Selection	1966	Asia Publishing House, Bombay
16	A Librarian Looks Back: An Autobiography	1992	ABC Pub. Hosue, New Delhi
17	New Education and School Libraries	2006	ESS P. (Delhi)/ Sarada Ranganathan Endowt, Bangalore

LIBRARY BOOKS PUBLICATIONS

S. No.	Books	Years	Authors	Born
1	Manual of Library Economy	1903	J.D. Brown	1862
2	Basic Statistics for Librarians	1975	I. Simpson	1927
3	Introduction to Librarianship	1968	J. K. Gates	1929
4	Documentation & Organiz. of Knowledge	1966	J.H. Shera	1903
5	Foundation of Education for Librarianship	1972	J.H. Shera	1903
6	Documentation and information	1983	B. Guha	1975
7	Documentation	1948	S. C. Bradford	1878
8	Communications	1990	J. Thompson	1856
9	Library Glossary & Reference books	1971	L.M. Harrold	1861
10	Little Science Big Science	1963	Derek John de Solla Price	1922
11	Putting Knowledge to work	1973	Pauline Atherton	1929
12	India's National Library	1961	B.S. Keshavan	1909
13	American Library Association	1876	Melvil Dewey	1851

14	American Metric Bureau	1876	Melvil Dewey	1851
15	World's First library school Columbia Univ. New York	1877	Melville Louis Kossuth Dewey	1851
16	Library journal (Boston, USA)	1877	Melvil Dewey	1851
17	National Bureau of Standards	1901	Melvil Dewey	1851
18	Encyclopedia of Library &info Sc.	1968	Allen Kent	1921

LIBRARY MOVEMENTS IN INDIA

S. No.	Founders	Born	Library Movements	Years
1	B.S. Keshavan	1909	National Library in India	1948
2	J.W. Borden	1810	Library of Baroda state, Gujarat	1911
3	G. Bhattacharya	1937	DRTC	1962
4	K.M. Asuddola	1890	Imperial Library	1930
5	Lord Curzon	1859	National Library	1903
6	Dr. S.R. Rangnathan	1892	School of Librarianship (india)	1929
7	P.N. Kaula	1924	B.H. University (1958 Librarian)	1916
8	A.D. Dickinson	1876	Punjab Government	1915
9	Siyaji Rao Gaikwad-3	1863	Library Movement-Baroda state	1910
10	D.S. Kothari	1928	U.G.C.	1953
11	Neena E. Browne	1860	Circulation System	1895
12	George Boole	1815	Role Operators	1834
13	Melvil Dewey	1851	American school for library science , Columbia University in New York	1887
14	W.C.B. Sayer	1881	School of Librarianship of the University of London	1919

NATIONAL AND INTERNATIONAL LIBRARIES

S. No.	Library	Years	Places
1	Bibliotheca Nationale	1440	France

2	Saraswathi Mahal Library	1675	Tanjore, Tamil Nadu
3	Rampur Raja Library	1774	U. P.
4	Bengal Royal Asiatic Society Library	1784	Bengal
5	Library of Congress	1800	USA
6	Asiatic Society Library	1804	Bombay
7	Calcutta Public Library	1835	Calcutta
8	British Museum	1841	UK
9	Gaya Public Library	1855	Gaya
10	Long Library	1856	Rajkot
11	State Lenin Library	1862	Russia
12	Government Library	1867	Janagarh
13	Baroda State Library	1877	Baroda
14	Adyar Library	1886	Adyar
15	Connemara Public Library	1890	Chennai
16	Khudabaksha Oriental Library	1891	Patna, Bihar
17	Dahi Laxmi Library	1892	Nadiad
18	Maharajah's Public Library	1899	Jaipur, Rajasthan
19	National Library, Germany	1912	Germany
20	National Medical Library	1947	New Delhi
21	National Library of India	1948	Calcutta
22	National Diet Library	1948	Japan
23	Delhi Public Library	1951	Delhi
24	National Science Library	1964	Delhi
25	Raja Rammohan Roy Library	1972	Calcutta
26	National Library for Blinds and Handicaps	1979	Dehradun
27	Medical Library Association of India (MLAI)	1980	New Delhi

LIST OF USERS THEIR PURPOSE

S. No.	Group of Users	Purpose
1	Students	For academic studies
2	Teaches	For imparting education
3	Professionals (Medical, Legal, Judicial, Etc.)	To pursue their Vocation
4	Engineers and technologists	For solving technical snags on

		industrial shop-floor
5	Business Managers, Top executives of Govt.	For decision making
6	Legislators	For arguing a point on the floor of the legislatures
7	Researchers	For their research work on a continuing basis

LIMITATIONS OF WORK PERIOD OF COPYRIGHT OF INDIA

S. N.	Author Works	Periods
1	Literary, Dramatic, Artistic or Musical Works	70 years end of the author dies
2	Computer generated works	50 years from the date of creation of work
3	Sound Recordings	50 years from the end of year in published
4	Broadcasts	50 years from the end of year of Broadcast
5	Typographical arrangement of published editions	25 years from the year of first publication
6	Design act	10 years
7	Copyright act	Life time author and After death 70 years
8	Trade mark act	10 years
9	Patent act	20 years
10	Geographical indication of goods act	10 years
11	Layout designs in integrated circuits	10 years

TYPES OF LIBRARIES

S. No.	Types	Examples
1.	Public Library	Saraswathi Mahal Library, Rampur Raja Library, Connemara Public Library, RRRLF, Khudabaksha Oriental Library etc.

2.	Academic Library	
2. (a)	School Library	DAV School library, Delhi Public School library etc.
2. (b)	College Library	GOVT. College Library, Ramjas College, Shyamlal College Library etc.
2. (c)	University Library	Deemed, States, Central Universities Libraries
3.	Special Library	National Science Library, National Library for Blind, Library of Supreme Court of India etc.
4.	National Library	National Library of India, British Library, Library of Congress etc.

RAJA RAM MOHAN ROY LIBRARY, 1972

S. N.	Publications	Library
1	Indian Libraries; Trends and Perspectives	RRRLF
2	Raja Rammohan Roy and the new learning	RRRLF
3	RRRLF Newsletter (Quarterly)	RRRLF
4	Directory of Indian public libraries	RRRLF
5	Granthana (Bi-annual)	RRRLF
6	Annual Report	RRRLF
7	'Books for the Millions at their Doorsteps'	RRRLF

LIBRARY LEGISLATIONS ACT IN INDIA (TAK MWMK HMG GOUR UCPBA)

S. No.	States Act	Years	Tax Provision
1	Tamil Nadu (Madras)	1948	Property/ House Tax (six Paise per Rupees)
2	Andhra Pradesh	1960	Property/ House Tax (Eight Paise per Rupees)
3	Karnataka	1965	Tax on Lands and Buildings
4	Maharashtra	1967	No Provision
5	West Bengal	1979	No Provision
6	Manipur	1988	No Provision
7	Kerala	1989	Building/ Property Tax (5 Paise per Rupees)
8	Haryana	1989	Property/ House Tax as decided

			by time to time Govt.
9	Mizoram	1993	No Provision
10	Goa	1993	Tax of 50 Paise per bulk liter of beer
11	Gujarat	2000	No Provision
12	Orissa	2001	No Provision
13	Uttarakhand	2005	No Provision
14	Rajasthan	2006	No Provision
15	Uttar Pradesh	2006	No Provision
16	Chhattisgarh	2009	No Provision
17	Pondicherry	2007	No Provision
18	Bihar	2008	No Provision
19	Arunachal Pradesh	2009	No Provision

COPYRIGHT ACTS / ORGANIZATIONS

S. No.	ACTs	Years	Places
1	The Patent Bill	1790	United States
2	American Patent Law	1810	United States
3	British Patent Law	1852	Great Britain
4	Intellectual Property Right Act	1856	Calcutta, India
5	Bern Conversation	1886	Switzerland
6	World intellectual Property Organization (WIPO)	1967	Geneva, Switzerland
7	The Design Act	1911	Great Britain
8	Universal Copyright Convention (UCC)	1952	Geneva, Switzerland
9	Berne Convention for the Protection of Literary	1971	Paris
10	The Copyright act	1957	India
11	Trade Marks Act	1958	India
12	The Patents Act	1970	India
13	Freedom of information Act	1982	India
14	WIPO Copyright Treaty	1996	Geneva, Switzerland
15	Telecom Act	1996	India
16	Digital Millennium Copyright Act	1998	India
17	Information Technology Act	2000	India
18	Communication Bill	2000	India

19	The Patent Law Treaty (PLT)	2000	Geneva, Switzerland
20	The Patent Cooperation Treaty	2001	Geneva, Switzerland
21	Internet Freedoms	2004	India
22	Right to information Act	2005	India
23	Video Franchise Bill	2006	India

COMMUNICATION MODELS

S. No.	Models	Founders	Years
1	Definition of Rhetoric	Aristotle	367–347 B.C.
2	Model of Proof	Aristotle	367–347 B.C.
3	Model of Communication / Verbal	Lasswell	1948
4	Mathematical Communication	Claude Shannon	1948
5	The Mathematical Model	Shannon Weaver	1949
6	Communication Model	Shanon Weaver	1949
7	Functional Model	Reusch and Bateson	1951
8	Interactive Model	Schramm	1954
9	Conceptual Model	Westley and Maclean	1957
10	S-M-C-R Model	Berlo	1960
11	English School of information	Colin Cherry	1961
12	Helical Spiral	Dance	1967
13	Rhetorical Situation	Bitzer	1968
14	Mosaic Model	Becker	1968
15	Transactional Model	Barnlund	1970
16	Systemic Model of Communication	Watzlawick	1972
17	Holographic Model	Brown	1987
18	Multistage Model of information	Charles Osgood	1987

INDIAN CONFERENCE OF LIBRARY

S. No.	Conferences	Places	Years
1	First Conference of Library Workers	Andhra Pradesh	1914
2	First Conference of Librarians	Lahore (Punjab)	1918
3	First All India Library Conference	Calcutta	1933
4	First All India Public Library Conference	Madras	1934

ANCIENT WRITING AND LIBRARIES

S. No.	Ancient Writing	Libraries
1	Palm leaves, birch barks, silk cloth, copper plates etc.	Indian Writing Materials
2	Clay tablets	Assyria and Babylonia (Sumerians)
3	Papyrus	Egyptian writing materials
4	Prisse Papyrus	Olds Book of Egyptians, saying of Ptahhotep
5	Handmade paper	China and India
6	Bone and paper	China
7	Vellum/ Parchment & wooden boards	Medieval Europe

INTERNATIONAL/NATIONAL LIBRARY ASSOCIATIONS

S. N.	Associations	Places	Years
1	ALA (American Library Association)	Chicago	1876
2	SLA(Special Libraries Association)	Washington	1909
3	LA (Library Association)	UK	1877
4	ASLIB(Association for information Management)	UK	1924
5	CILIP (Chartered institute of Library and information Professionals)	London	2002
6	ILA(Indian Library Association)	N. Delhi	1933
7	IASLIC (Indian Association of Special Libraries and Information Centre's)	Calcutta	1955
8	IATLIS (Indian Association of the	N. Delhi	1969

	Teachers of Library and Information Science)		
9	PLA - Public Library Association	ALA	1944

LIBRARY ASSOCIATION (STATE LEVEL) IN INDIA

S. N.	Associations	States	Years
1	Andhra Pradesh Library Association	Andhra Pradesh	1914
2	Maharashtra Library Association	Maharashtra	1921
3	West Bengal Library Association	West Bengal	1925
4	Madras Library Association	Madras	1928
5	Karnataka Library Association	Karnataka	1929
6	Punjab Library Association	Punjab	1929
7	Samastha Kerala Pustakalaya Samiti	Kerala	1931
8	Bihar Library Association	Bihar	1936
9	Assam Library Association	Assam	1938
10	Utkal Library Association	Odessa	1944
11	Kerala Library Association	Kerala	1945
12	Hyderabad Library Association	Andhra Pradesh	1951
13	U.P. Library Association	Utter Pradesh	1951
14	Delhi Library Association	Delhi	1953
15	Gujarat Library Association	Gujarat	1953
16	Madhya Bharat Library Association	Madhya Pradesh	1957
17	Gomantak Library Association	Karnataka	1961
18	Rajasthan Library Association	Rajasthan	1962
19	Jammu & Kashmir Library Association	Jammu & Kashmir	1966
20	Tripura Library Association	Tripura	1967
21	Haryana Library Association	Haryana	1975
22	Manipur Library Association	Manipur	1987
23	Mizoram Library Association	Mizoram	1987
24	Meghalaya Library Association	Meghalaya	1994
25	Nagaland Library Association	Nagaland	1996

TYPE OF LIBRARY AND MEANINGS

S. N.	Libraries	Meanings
1	Public	A free informational and recreational

	Library	institution. Its mission is to provide reading materials to people without any fee.
2	Academic Library	The libraries that are attached with educational institutions are known as academic library.
3	National Library	The mission is to preserve the cultural heritage of a Nation.
4	Special Library	Libraries attached to special institution i.e. industrial firm, insurance company, All India Radio, Dordarshan Kendra, etc.
5	Personal/ Private Library	A library owned by an individual or family with reading materials collected, maintained and intended to be used by a family.
6	Archives	An organized collection of the noncurrent records of an institution, government, or corporate body, preserved in a repository for their historical value.
7	Library (Tradition al)	The collection of the traditional libraries is mostly print material; manuscripts etc and the collections are not well organized.
8	Automate d Library	A library with machine-readable catalogues, computerized acquisition, circulation and OPAC are called as automated library.
9	Electronic Library	When an automated library goes for Local Area Networking (LAN) and CD-ROM networking then it is known as electronic library.
10	Digital Library	The Digital Library (DL) is a later stage of electronic library. When an electronic library started procuring e-journal and access is over the web, then it is termed as digital library.
11	Virtual Library	Virtual Library is the scientifically managed collection of information resources and services on site as well as off site that are available in a virtual reality environment and any geographical location.
12	Hybrid Library	The libraries, which are working both in electronic or digital and print environment, are known as hybrid library.

FIVE LAW OF LIBRARY SCIENCE = 1931 DR. S. R. RANGNATHAN

S. No.	Laws	Explains
1	Books are for use	Place, Hour, Staff, Furniture and Building location to easy accessibility of the library to its users.
2	Every reader his/her book	Obligation of the staff and reader, choice of staff and resource sharing.
3	Every book its reader	One method involved the basic rules for access to the collection, most notably the need for open shelving and arrangement, eye catching to reader.
4	Save the time of the reader	Only include those who possess strong reference skills, but also strong technical skills in cataloging, cross-referencing, ordering, accessioning, and the circulation of materials.
5	Library is a growing organism	The growth in staff, the physical collection, and patron use.

MAJOR LIBRARY SECTIONS

S.N.	Sections	Explains
1	Acquisition Section	This section is responsible for building up the library collection.
2	Technical Section	The department has three distinct functions: classification, cataloguing and physical processing.
3	Circulation Section	The main function of the circulation section is charging and discharging of books.
4	Reference Section	The nature and level of reference service varies with the nature and size of a library.
5	Periodicals Section	Different libraries have different system for organizing acquisition and maintenance of periodicals. Libraries with large number of serials' subscription organise the entire routines in an independent section.
6	Maintenance Section	The section is primarily concerned with upkeep and maintenance of library materials in good

		conditions.
7	Administration Section	The administration section looks after the administrative activities of a library which involves library manpower, finance and accounts, library building, library assets such as furniture and equipments.
8	Theses & Dissert.	The Theses Section is the repository of the under-graduate, graduate and doctorate works of the university.
9	Text Book Section	This section is situated in Ground Floor and only manages text books in different stacks of the library subject-wise.
10	Networking section	The refers to a interconnected platform of some group of libraries with certain agreements aims to satisfy and fulfill their users' need.

LIBRARY SOCIETY TERMS

S. N.	Library Terms	Year	Explains
1	A Bibliography Written By	1944	Ferment Rider
2	A Library is A Public Institution Or Establishment Charged With The Care of Collection of Books, The duty of making them accessible to those who require the use of them and the task of converting every person in its neighborhood into a habitual library goers and reader of books		Dr S R Rangnathan
3	Abburi Shiyali research awards		Best LIS Research
4	Accession Register Record is		Húb of the stack in a library
5	AGBILA (Quarterly) Stands for	1949	Annals, Bulletin and Grandhalay of Indian Library Association
6	Aligarh Muslim University the		BLIS Course Started

	first University in India by		
7	Alvin Toffler and John Naisbitt		USA 1970
8	Andhra University started by	1935	Certificate Course
9	ASK (Approach, Skill, Knowledge) Principle is		Management
10	ASLIB was acquired by MCB group	2010	Emerald publishing
11	BSO in classification stands		Broad Subject Ordering
12	Calcutta Public Library was Established During 19th Century	1836	Maharaja Sayajirao Gaekwad
13	CALIBER Stands for		Convention on automation of libraries in education and research institutions, INFLIBNET
14	Classification Of All Types Of Libraries		UNESCO
15	Committee on National Policy on Library and Information System (CONPOLIS)	1986	RRLF By Dept Of Culture
16	Communication Barrier		Noise
17	Communication channel		Formal & informal
18	Communication Medium		Radio
19	Communication mode Shannon and weaver information is	1948	BIT, (Sender, Channel, Message, Receiver and feedback)
20	Concretes and Processes was given		S. R. Rangnathan
21	Connecting people and information		SLA, Viginia -1909
22	COPSAT stands for		Current Online Patent in Science and Technology
23	Delhi University established by	1947	PG Diploma Course in LIS
24	Data, information, Knowledge, Wisdom		Logical sequence

25	Delivery of books and newspaper act	1954	
26	Descriptive Information is		Encyclopedia
27	Document		Physical carrier of information
28	Dr. Umpathi fellowship for		LIS Students
29	Entropy		Information for doing useful work
30	Fair use		Copy right
31	Five laws of library science	1931	Meenakshi college, Annamalainag r
32	Growth of Libraries		5th law
33	H.Q. of FID was shifted from Brussels	1934	The Hague
34	Handling of information		Information Industry
35	High Level Language is		Machine independent
36	IASLIC Bulletin Published	1955	Quarterly, Calcutta
37	IATLIS Moti Wala Award		Best Teachers
38	IATLIS Ratna Laxman Rao award for		Women Professionals
39	ILA Kaula award for	1933	Best Librarian
40	ILA member of IFLA	1957	
41	India awards teachers in LIS		IATLIS
42	Indian Library Science	1967	Quarterly, New Delhi
43	Informal communication/ knowledgeable person		Invisible College
44	Informal self education is		Public Library
45	Information		Organized Data
46	Information Categorized into 3 type		Statistical, Descriptive and Analytical
47	Information science	1959	
48	Information Science added to Librarianship	1950	
49	Information Society		MaSuda, Japan
50	Information Transfer		Beesman
51	Int. inst. of Documentation changed	1937	Int. Federation of Documentation

52	International Information System on Research in Documentation		UNESCO (NATIS) National Information System
53	Invisible web refers to part of internet		Hidden from search
54	ISBD and Cataloguing Codes		Bibliographic Description
55	ISBN office shifted from Kolkata to Delhi	2011	
56	It is "a Library With Little or no Physical Presence of Books, Periodicals, Reading Space or Support Staff, But are that disseminate selective information directly to distribute library customers, usually electronically"		Powell
57	Journal International Classification Pub.		ISKO
58	Librarianship is not a profession		Madden, Moon, Moore, Mc Pheron
59	Library and information Policy in India		RRRLF-1972
60	Library Association to form CILIP	2002	Institute of information Scientists
61	Library Legislation refers to		Development of Pubic Library
62	Library Technology Report Pub.		ALA
63	Library Week Celebrated 14th To 20th November	1968	The Memories of Pandit Jawharla Nehru Annually Since
64	Managing information		ASLIB
65	Meaning of 'Translation Pools' is		Translation Experts
66	National Centre For Bibliometrics		INSDOC, New Delhi
67	Polytechnics in Delhi, Chandigarh and Bangalore	1960	Diploma Library Science

68	PV.Varghese Prize for		Best Article Published In ILA
69	Resource sharing is part of		Library cooperation
70	RRRLF Was Established	1972	Culcutta, ISBN, Govt. Of India
71	Reading Centre's, story hours, exhibitions and reading to literature are		Service of extension/ public library
72	S.R. Rangnathan Five Laws Of Library Science (1931)	1931	1) Books are for use (Location of library, hour of library) 2) Every Reader his/her book (Obligation) 3) Every Books its reader (Arrangement) 4) Save the time of the reader 5) Library is a growing organism
73	S.R.Ranganathan Autobiography		"A Librarian Looks Back"
74	Section of the library is known as		Hub of the staff technical section
75	Shelf List facilitates		Stock verification
76	Sixth law "Every reader his/her freedom"	2010	James R. Retting
77	Society for Information Science (SIS)	1976	New Delhi
78	Staffing is		Maintaining of Human Resources
79	Stochastic Equation of Information Solved		General Equilibrium
80	Suggested for book order vigilance pad		S. R. Rangnathan
81	Tagging in Web 2.0 Application is called		Syndication /Directory
82	Term 'Bibliophile' Refers		Book Lover
83	The 'Acronym' by	1946	UNESCO

84	The "Sister libraries" for children`s		IFLA
85	The 1920 Training program at Bangalore by		Mysore Sir. M. Vishweswaraiah
86	The "Universal Availability of Publication" Program	1972	IFLA
87	The Canadian Library Association	1946	
88	The "Special Libraries serve a specialist cliental, located within a single establishment or group and all engaged in working towards one common purpose."		R. Astall
89	The Farmington Plan is		Library Cooperation
90	The 'Five Laws of Library Science'	1931	Applied or Basic Research
91	The Government of India awards Padmashree to Rangnathan	1965	Valuable Contribution In Library Science
92	The term 'Kinesis' is Related		Communication
93	The Transmission of receiver's reaction back to the sender is		Feedback
94	Tom Stonier, and Daniel Bell (second)		(1980)
95	UNESCO Assisted Model Public Library in India		Delhi
96	Unit of information		Byte
97	Universal Availability of Publications	1970	IFLA- Closed-2003
98	University of Madras started by	1936	Diploma Course
99	Vedanvayaki Fellowship for		MLIS Students
100	W. A. Borden start is	1910	Refresher Course for librarians in India

2

Library Management

MANAGEMENT THEORIES AND FOUNDERS

S. N.	Theories	Years	Founders	Birth
1	Father of Scientific Management Principals		F.W. Taylor	1856
2	Rules of Thumb Method		F.W. Taylor	1856
3	Scientific Method of Management		F.W. Taylor	1856
4	Functions of Management		Henry Fayol	1841
5	Father of Modern Management		Henry Fayol	1841
6	Management By Objective	1950	Peter Drucker	1909
7	Best Way to Predict The Future is to Create		Peter Drucker	1909
8	Leadership is Doing The Right Things		Peter Drucker	1909
9	Management as a Discipline	1954	Peter Drucker	1909
10	Hierarchy of Need Theory		A. Maslow	1908
11	Theory X And Theory Y	1950	D. McGregor	1906
12	Style of Leadership		D. McGregor	1906
13	Motivation- Hygiene Approach		Frederick Herzberg	1923
14	Psychological Factors	1908	Hugo Munsterberg	1863
15	Human Emotions	1892	Mary Parker Follett	1868
16	Hawthorne Studies	1928	Elton Mayo	1880
17	Sociological Perspective		Elton Mayo	1880
18	Human Relations Theory School		Elton Mayo	1880

19	Human Relations Approach		Elton Mayo	1880
20	Humanistic Theory of Learning	1949	Carl Rogers	1902
21	Task and Bonus		Henry Grant	1861
22	Bureastic Model / System School		Max Weber	1864
23	Bureaucratic Organization		Max Weber	1864
24	Bureaucracy Theory School		Max Weber	1864
25	Contingency Style	1960	Fred Fiedler	1922
26	Hierarchy of Needs	1943	Abraham Maslow	1880
27	Motivational Theory		Abraham Maslow	1880
28	Theory of Human Motivation		Abraham Maslow	1880
29	General System Theory	1968	Von Bertalanffy	1901
30	Theory Z	1980	William Ouchi	1943
31	Goal-Setting Theory	1960	Edwin A. Loc ke	1938
32	Pyramid Concept	1998	Prahalad C.K.	1941
33	Improvement in Human Machines	--------	Robert Owen	1771
34	4 Styles of Leadership	1967	Rensis Likert	1903
35	Reflections on Leadership	1967	Rensis Likert	1903
36	Leadership & Management	1967	Rensis Likert	1903
37	Principal of Supportive Relationship		Rensis Likert	1903
38	Pyramid Shape of Organizational Control		Portrays	1915
39	Fitness For Use	1950	Joseph Mose s Juran	1904
40	Decision Theory School Theory	1948	Herbert Simo n	1916
41	7 Principal Total Quality Management	1987	William E. Deming	1900
42	14 Principal of Management	1888	Henry Fayol	1841
43	27 Principles of Management.	1960	George Terry	1950

44	29 General Principles of Administration	1943	Lyndall Urwick	1891
45	52 Principles of Management	2006	Harold Koontzs	1909
46	Management Process School Theory		Harold Koontzs	1909
47	Management Jungle Theory	1965	Harold Koontzs	1909
48	Simple Random Sampling		Lottery Method	
49	Simple Random Number Table		Systematic Number	
50	Stratified Random Number Table		Systematic Groups	
51	Cluster Sampling		Multistage	
52	Total Quality Management (Japan)	1950	William E. Deming	1900
53	Control of Quality /	1971	William E. Deming	1900
54	Six Sigma (Motorola, USA)	1981	Bill Smith	1929
55	Managerial Grid	1950	R. Blake/ J. Mouton	1918

HENRY FAYOL (1841)

S. No.	14 Principals (1888)
1	Division of Work
2	Authority
3	Discipline
4	Unity of Command
5	Unity of Direction
6	Subordination of individual interests to general interest
7	Remuneration
8	Centralization
9	Scalar Chain
10	Order
11	Equity
12	Stability of Tenure of Personnel
13	Initiative

14	Esprits De Corps

IFLA — INTERNATIONAL FEDERATION OF LIBRARY ASSOCIATIONS AND INSTITUTIONS-1927 (THE HAGUE, NETHERLANDS)

S. No.	Programs (IFLA)	Years
1	ISBD (international Standard Bibliographic Description)	1971
2	ISBD (Monographic)	1974
3	ISBD(General)	1977
4	ISBD (Antiquarian)	1980
5	ISBD (Printed Music)	1980
6	ISBD(non-book materials)	1981
7	ISBD(Serials)	1981
8	ISBD (cartographic materials)	1981
9	ISBD (Computer files)	1990
10	ISBD (Electronic Resources merge CF)	1997
11	ISBD (Continuing Resources)	2002
12	IMCE (international Meeting of Cataloguing Experts), Copenhagen	1969
13	UBC (Universal Bibliographic Control)	1974
14	UAP (Universal Availability of Publications)	1976
15	UNIMARC (*Universal* Machine Readable Cataloging)	1977
16	(PAC) Preservation and Conservation	1984
17	FRBR (Functional Requirements for Bibliographic Records)	1998
18	UNIMARC Strategic Programme	2003
19	FRAD (Functional Requirements for Authority Data)	2009
20	FRSAD (Functional Requirements for Subject Authority Data)	2010
21	RDA (Resource Description & Access)	2010
22	BSLA (Building Strong Library Associations)	2012
23	(LDP) Library Development Programme	2017
24	(FAIFE) Freedom of Access to information and Freedom of Expression	2018
25	(CLM)Copyright and other Legal Matters	2019

AMERICAN LIBRARY ASSOCIATION-1876 (CHICAGO AND WASHINGTON, D.C., UNITED STATES)

S. No.	Programs (ALA)	Years
1	AACR-I	1967
2	AACR-II	1978
3	Sears List of Subject Headings 1st Ed.	1923
4	SLSH 17st Ed. (H. W. Wilson)	2000
5	SLSH 19st Ed. (H. W. Wilson)	2007
6	SLSH 20st Ed. (H. W. Wilson)	2010
7	SLSH 21st Ed. (EBSCO)	2014
8	SLSH 22st Ed. (H.W. Wilson; 22 edition (July 23, 2018))	2018
9	RDA(Resource Description and Access)	2010

LIBRARY OF CONGRESS -1800 (WASHINGTON, D.C., UNITED STATES

S. No.	Programs (Library of Congress)	Years
1	MARC (Machine-Readable Cataloging)	1960
2	MARC-1	1966
3	MARC-11	1968
4	RETRO CONVERSION	1969
5	LCSH 1st Ed.	1911
6	LCSH 7st Ed.	1966
7	LCSH 8TH Ed.	1975
8	LCSH 36TH	2014
9	LCSH 37TH	2015
10	LCSH 38TH	2016
11	LCSH 39TH (April)	2017
12	LCSH 40TH (January)	2018
13	LCSH 41TH (March)	2019

14	MARC-21 (Z.39.2) (ISO 2709)	1999
15	Z39.50	1973
16	Bibliographic Frame	1960
17	EAD, Encoded Archival Description (XML)	1998
18	Metadata Authority Description Schema(MADS)	2015
19	Extended Date/Time Format (EDTF)	2019

UNITED NATIONS EDUCATIONAL, SCIENTIFIC AND CULTURAL ORGANIZATION-1946 (PARIS, FRANCE)

S. No.	Programs (UNESCO)	Years
1	Common Communication Format Sponsored	1978
2	CCF 1st Pub.	1984
3	CCF 2nd Pub.	1988
4	World Programme for Human Rights Education (WPHRE)	2004
5	Information for All Programme (IFAP)	2007
6	General information programme (PGI)	1978
7	United Nations international Scientific information System (UNISIST)	1971
8	'Data retrieval systems for the social and human sciences' DARE	1972

COMMISSION AND COMMITTEES IN INDIA

S. N.	Commission	Years	Founders
1	Hunter Education Commission	1882	Sir William Hunter
2	Indian University Commission	1902	Lord Curzen
3	Sadler Commission, Calcutta University	1917	Sadler
4	Fayzee Commission	1939	Library development committee
5	Radhakrishanan Committee / University Education Commission	1948	Sarvepalli Radhakrishnan
6	Secondary Education Commission	1953	Dr. A. L. Mudaliar

7	University Grants Commission (Government of India)	1953	Maulana Abul Kalam Azad
8	Education Commission	1964	Prof. D. S. Kothari
9	New Education Policy	1986	Government of india
10	National Knowledge Commission	2005	Dr. Manmohan Singh
11	Riche committee	1926	Library Science
12	Statham Committee	1932	Library Funds
13	Sarkar Committee	1945	Technical Education in india
14	Bhatnagar Committee	1947	Scientists, Technologists, Engineers & Doctors
15	Library Committee	1957	Dr. S. R. Ranganathan
16	Lal Committee	1957	M. Library and inf. Science
17	Library Advisory Committee	1958	K.P. Sinha
18	Thacker Committee	1959	Postgraduate Engineering Education and Research
19	Review Committee on Library Science	1961	Dr. S. R. Ranganathan
20	Yash Pal Committee	1970	Science and Technology
21	Damodaran Committee	1970	Polytechnic Education
22	Chandrakant Committee	1971	Postgraduate Education and Research Programmes
23	Kelkar Committee	1976	Polytechnic institutions and Teachers for Polytechnics
24	Jha Committee	1978	Staff Structure for

			Technical Teachers' Training institutes
25	Nayudamma Committee	1978	PG Education and Research in Engineering and Technology
26	Mehrotra Committee	1983	R. C. Mehrotra
27	Committee on National Network System for University Libraries	1988	Yash Pal
28	Curriculum Devpt. Committee on LIS	1990	Prof. P. N. Kaula
29	A. Bhattacharya Review Committee	1991	Technical Teachers Training Inst.
30	P Rama Rao Committee	1995	PG Education and Research in Engineering & Technology
31	Mashelkar Committee	1996	Regional Engineering Colleges
32	UGC Model Curriculum: Library and Information Science	2001	Dr. C.R. Karisiddappa
33	U.R. Rao Committee	2002	Review the Functioning of AICTE
34	Dr Anil Kakodkar Committee	2010	New IITs/ IIMs and Improving
35	National Mission on Libraries	2012	National Knowledge Commission
36	Adams Report	1915	Cooperative Library Programs
37	Mitchell & Kenyon Report	1924	Library Service
38	Mc Colvin Report	1942	Public Library System
39	Robert Report	1959	Commercial Education in The Secondary Schools

40	UGC-UK (Parry Committee Report)	1964	University Libraries

TOTAL QUALITY MANAGEMENT (SEVEN TOOLS, 1960) FISHBONE AND KAORU ISHIKAWA (1915-89)

S. N.	Charts	Expiations
1	Ishikawa Diagram	Problem and sorts ideas into useful categories.
2	Check Sheet	A Structured, Prepared form for collecting and analyzing data.
3	Control Chart	Graph used to study how a process changes over time. data are plotted in time order.
4	Histogram	A Histogram is the most commonly used graph to show frequency distributions.
5	Pareto Chart	A Pareto Chart is a length of the bars graph represents frequency.
6	Scatter Diagram	Graphs Pairs of numerical data, one variable on each axis, to look for a relationship.
7	Flowchart or Run Chart	Technique that separates data gathered from variety of sources.

T.D. WILSON, 1981 (INFORMATION SEEKING BEHAVIOUR MODELS) UNITED KINGDOM

S. N.	Stages	Process
1	Starting	The characteristic of the initial search for information.
2	Chaining	The information seeker follows the chains of citations.
3	Browsing	A semi-directed searching in an area of potential interest.
4	Differentiating	Characterized by activities in which the user ranks the information sources.
5	Monitoring	Similar to searching for the information for current awareness purposes.
6	Filtering	The use of certain criteria when searching for

		information to make the information as relevant.
7	Extracting	The user systematically works through a particular source to locate material of interest in the extracting mode.
8	Ending	The 'tying up the loose ends' through a final search.

D. ELLIS, 1989 (INFORMATION SEEKING BEHAVIOUR MODELS) AUSTRALIA

S. N.	Stages	Process
1	Starting	The characteristic of the initial search for information.
2	Chaining	The information seeker follows the chains of citations.
3	Browsing	A semi-directed searching in an area of potential interest.
4	Differentiating	Characterized by activities in which the user ranks the information sources.
5	Monitoring	Similar to searching for the information for current awareness purposes.
6	Extracting	The user systematically works through a particular source to locate material of interest in the extracting mode.

C. KUHLTHAU, 1991 (INFORMATION SEEKING BEHAVIOUR MODELS) UNITED STATES

S. N.	Stages	Process
1	Initiation	When a person comes to know the lack of knowledge.
2	Selection	The uncertainty on the area, topic or problem is not cleared.
3	Exploration	While exploring for information people will get doubt on the consistency of the information.
4	Formulation	The person gets focused perception which leads to clarity.

5	Collection	The right direction, information related to the focused perspective is gathered.
6	Presentation	After the completion of the search the seeker gets new knowledge.

BASIC PRINCIPLES OF LIBRARY BUILDING DESIGN

S.N.	Designs	Structure
1	Functional Design	Library building should have functional design rather than a monumental one and provision for documents, users, staff, and service areas.
2	Open Access	The availability of the number of library staff, the user demand and the type of collection are deciding factors for open access system.
3	Future Growth	Library building should be planned for at least next 20 years, keeping in view the rate of collection development, readers, etc.
4	Flexible	There should be the means of interchangeability of all major stack areas, service areas, reading room, and staff areas.
5	Air-conditioning, Lighting and Noise	Uniform standards of lighting, heating, cooling, ventilation, noise prevention, communications, fumigation and flooring are necessary to meet the criteria of interchangeability.
6	Modular Design	A building on modular system is the one which is supported by columns placed at regular interval.
7	Economic	The design should be such that the operation of the library can be carried out with the minimum of staff and finance.
8	Secure	The building should be free from dust, dirt, and cobwebs.

B. DERVIN, 1983 (INFORMATION SEEKING BEHAVIOUR MODELS) UNITED STATES

S. N.	Stages	Process
1	Situation	The time and space, which defines the context in which information problems arise.
2	Time/ Space Gap	A gap, which identifies the difference between the contextual situation and the desired situation.
3	Outcome	The consequences of the sense-making process.
4	Bridge	The means of closing the gap between situation and outcome.

BOOK SELECTION THEORIES

S.N.	Theories	Founder	Years
1	Theory of Book Selection	L. R. McColvin	1925
2	Book Selection	Drury	1930
3	Living with book	Haines	1935
4	Library book selection	Ranganathan	1952
5	Selecting Materials for Libraries	Rovert Broadus	1981
6	Building Library Collections	Arthur Curley, Dorothy M. Broderick	1985
7	Select the best documents within the finance available	Dewey's Principle	

STACK MAINTENANCE

The maintenance work implies the organization of stack rooms, arrangements of books on shelve in stack rooms and conservation: Preparation maintenance of guides, Shelf rectification, shelf register/list, routines, and tools needed in the maintenance section.

STACK GUIDES

S. N.	Guides	Maintenance
(1)	Tier Guide	Each tier of stacks should have one tier guide showing the arrangement of books on the shelves in that tier.

(2)	Gangway Guide	Each gangway should be provided with a gangway guide, indicating the subjects covered in the particular gangway with help of class numbers.
(3)	Bay Guide	Every bay of shelves be provided with a bay guide containing the concerned class numbers and their verbal headings.
(4)	Shelf Guide	Every shelf should be provided with a shelf guide giving the class numbers to denote the subject on which the books are found in a particular shelf.
(5)	General Guide	A guide giving an overall view of the stacks and the arrangement of books has to be provided preferably in the lobby or somewhere near the entrance.
(6)	General instruction	The maintenance section should provides : No Smoking Please, Talk and Walk Softly, Silence Please and Do not shelve the books etc.

SHELF REGISTER/SHELF LIST

Shelf register or shelf list is an important record of books; which shows the position of any book on the shelves. in order to control the movement of books in a library a shelf list is, made use of. A shelf list is usually maintained in standard size cards. These cards are arranged parallel to the corresponding arrangement of books on the shelves.

MAINTENANCE ROUTINE

The shelf arrangement and stock verification, the maintenance section/division should also attend to day-to-day routines. The duties of routine maintenance work are the following:

1	Dusting and Cleaning of Shelves	These are important and indispensable routines of libraries which have to be attended meticulously. Books have to be protected from dust and dirt.
2	Shelving	Books received from the processing sections of the library need to be displayed for a week or ten days on the latest additions shelf, before are taken to the stacks for shelving.

3	Shelf Study and Shelf Rectification	The maintenance staff at all levels in a library would do well to devote their free time to studying the books on the shelves so as to develop a fair knowledge of their contents.
4	Damaged Books	Shelf study and shelf rectification would also enable the maintenance staff to identify books that need mending, etc.
5	Shifting and Resifting Books	In order to take away the monotony of appearance of shelf arrangement and to introduce an element of novelty, books have to be reshuffled to keep in tune with the changing popularity of subjects with the reading public.
6	Assistance to Readers	Readers often need advice and help in locating and identifying books of their interest.
7	Maintenance of Book Tags	Book tags carry call number of books fixed at the bottom of books or on their spines. This helps the arrangement of books on the shelf.

TOOLS
The maintenance section needs to be provided with the following tools: (1) Books ends or book supporters (2) Book lifts and trollies (3) Shelving tables (4) A number of stools for short persons to browse books kept on top shelves and also for easy replacement of the books.(5) Two step or three step ladders for reaching upper shelves for shelving, cleaning and dusting.

INTERNATIONAL ORGANIZATION FOR STANDARDIZATION, (OSI) IN 1977 (ISO MODEL 7 LAYERS, PDNTSPA)

S. No.	Layers	Termlogy
1	Physical layer	Transmits Bit Stream to Physical Medium
2	Data line layer	Provides Data Exchange Between Devices on the Same Medium
3	Network layer	Takes Care of Switches and Routes information Units
4	Transport layer	Provides Reliable end-to-end Data Transmission

5	Session layer	Maintains Dialogue Between Communication Devices
6	Presentation layer	Formats Data (Ex: ASCII)
7	Application layer	Provides General Services Related to Applications

METHODS SCALES

S. N.	Scales	Explains	Founder	Years
1	Thurstone Scales	Group of Judgments	Thurstone	1928
2	Likert Scales	Graded Structure	Rensis Likert	1932
3	Interval Scales	Equal Units of Measurement	Paul Velleman	1940
4	Semantic differential Scales	Opposite Positions	C.E. Osgood	1957

LIBRARY MANAGEMENT TERMS

S. N.	Library terms	Year	Explains
1	A Bounded Book which consists of		Blank Book
2	A Committee on national network of libraries was started	1988	
3	A Publication title page is missing is called_		Anepigraphon
4	A Small Book is technically called_		Biblot
5	A Technique for identifying the theme of a document from its citations is		Bibliographic Coupling
6	A title disclosed The Subject of document is		Binders title
7	A "Gazette" gives information		Official announcement and notifications
8	Accession List South Asia		Us Library Of

	(Monthly)		Congress, New Delhi
9	Accession Register is		Records of circulation section
10	Agglomeration in		Mutually and exclusively related are agglomerated or grouped together to form into a single group (E.G. Social Science, Natural Science)
11	ALA has prescribed		Standards for library binding
12	An Entry that is made for the subject of a chapter in a book is		Book Index Entry
13	Anomalous State of Knowledge proposed by		J.N. Belkin
14	Astrophysics is a result of		Fusion
15	Auto Charging first introduced	1934	St Louris
16	Barriers of Communication		Noise, Language, Over Production
17	Bibliographies are used to find information is		Subject Documents
18	Bibliomentry is		Information Management
19	BISNET was launched by FICCI to		Wide variety of business inf. service
20	Books back from the users and releasing the borrower's ticket is		Discharging
21	Books misplaced on the shelves by readers are restored		Shelf Rectification
22	Building Expenditure is		Capital Expenditure
23	Building Library collection		Acquisition
24	C.A. Cutter coined		Author mark in classification number
25	Canon of Recall Value is the another name		Canon of Sought Headings

26	CD -Rom	1985	Philips & Sony Company
27	Central Drug Research Institute		Pune
28	Central Salt and Marine Chemical Research Institute		Bhubaneswar
29	Chain Index		Helps to prepared class index entry
30	Channels of Info. Communication		Formal- Articles, Research Report's, Books. Informal- Conversation, Informal Discussion.
31	Chronemics_that is to		Time is considered is sometimes a message in itself, a form of non-verbal communication
32	Class Index Entry in CCC is known as		Subject Analytical Entry
33	Cluster		Ideology, Sinology, Etc.
34	CODEN was designed by		Charles Bishop
35	Computer Mouse was invented by		Douglas Engel hand
36	Concept of Feedback is found in		System Approach
37	Conference		A Student and her adviser
38	Controlled Groups Is A Term Is Used		Experimental Research
39	CPM - Critical Path Method	1957	DuPont Network Model For Project
40	CRG Stands (Classification Research Group)	1952	J. Mills, London (Information Retrieval)
41	Critical Incident Techniques is one type of		Observation Method

42	Cross References is		A Space saver and serves to prevent duplication
43	Current Awareness Service has come in	1950	
44	DEC stand for		Data Evolution Centre
45	Decachotomy		Division into ten DDC
46	Decent Indian Books (Quarterly)		Federation of Indian Publishers, New Delhi
47	Delegation of Authority means		Decentralization of power among library staff
48	Dichotomy		Division Into Two
49	Distillation		Pure Subject distilled or emerged out of combination of different compound subject-Management, Statistical Calculus, Microbiology
50	Dizo Copying is a method of		Photographic Reprographic Service
51	Dublin Core Meta Data consist of		17 Elements
52	E.C. Richardson defined notation as		Short and Sign
53	E.C. Richardson is author of book		Classification : Theoretical and practical
54	E.J. Coats invented		Retroactive Ordinal Notation
55	E-Choupal is a initiatives Launched		ITC
56	EFTS Stands For		Electronic Fund

			Transfer System
57	E-Gyankosh are protected by		IGNOU
58	Electronic Society	1970	Zblgnlew Brozozinski
59	E-Zine is a term used		Electronic Magazine
60	Father of Classical School		Henri Fayol
61	Feature of an information retrieval system		Relevance, Precision and Recall
62	Fiber Optical is used in		Telecommunication
63	Fielder's Theory of Leadership is		Contingency Model
64	First Global Information System	1969	International Nuclear Information System
65	First Library Journal in India		Indian Library Journal
66	Flow Chart		A Graph picture that shows program logic
67	Four entity of FRBR model are		Work, Expression, Manifestation, Item
68	Francis Bacon said		'Some books are to be tasted, others to be swallowed and some few to be chewed and digested'
69	Fusion		Two more than two subject fused together (Biology + Physics = Biophysics)
70	Geodata and Information Division		Kolkata
71	'GMD' is stands for		General Material Designation
72	Guide to Literature come under		Tertiary Sources
73	Haptics which refers to		The Use of touch to communicate, for example, shaking hands, holding hands, patting.
74	Hard Disk are also called as		Winchester Disk

75	Herald of Library Science-Lucknow	1962	P.N. Kaula
76	In CC LED stands for		Latest Effective Decade
77	In CC, "O: (Literature) Stands		Language, Form, Author, Work
78	In the title "Prevention of lung disease in India" the personality is		Lung
79	Ind Cat is a Union Catalogue of Indian Universities compiled by		INFLIBNET
80	INDEST is a consortia located	2003	New Delhi
81	Indian Book Industry (Monthly)		Sterling Publishers Pvt. Ltd,
82	Indian Cultural Heritage		IGNCA
83	Indian Library review launched by	2011	National Library, Calcutta
84	Indian National Bibliography (Monthly)		Central Reference Library, Kolkata
85	Informatics coined by	1979	Otto Nacke
86	Information Desk		Reference Service
87	Information Retrieval Coined	1950	Calvin Moors
88	Information Society concept	1966	Japan "Johoka Shakal"
89	Information Systems and decision science (ISDS)		ROME
90	INFOTERRA established	1972	Sweden
91	Internal Colleague with external sources of information is		Technology Gatekeeper
92	ISBN (International Standard Book Number) changed from 10 digits to 13 from	2007	In 2011 The ISBN Calcutta To Delhi
93	ISBN Contains 13 Digit number of		5 Parts- 1st Group Identification, 2nd Publisher, 3rd Title Identifier, 4th Check Digit, 5th EAN (European Article Number)

94	ISSN consist of (Parris)	1975	8 Digits, Journals (first digit represents name of publisher and last digit represents check digit)
95	J. Martine defined information is		Product and Process
96	J.D. Brown was published journal		The Library World (Monthly)
97	JCCC stands for (A P J Abdul Kalam)	2003	J-Gate Custom Content Consortia UGC- Infonet Digital Library Consortium
98	Job Description refers to		Analysis of a given job into different levels
99	Job Evolution		Ranking, Classification, Factor Comparison, Point System Method
100	Kinesics includes		Facial Expressions, Eye Movements, Gestures
101	Knowledge Society	1969	Peter Ducker
102	Krishikosh	2012	State Agricultural Universities. New Delhi
103	Lamination		Constructed by overlaying facet on facet, even as we make -agriculture in India
104	Largest Gazetteer of The World		The Time Index
105	LC marks service began with		US Imprints
106	Library and information science journal name reference reviews		ASLIB book guide
107	Library Catalogue Cards designed called		Catalogue Cabinet is size 23" * 28"

108	Library Committee is		Statutory Committee
109	Library, Entering the personal belongings of a reader is		Property Counter
110	Likert Name is associated with		Style of leadership
111	Luther Gluck, Terms POSDCORB	.	Planning, Organizing, Staffing, Directing, Coordinating, Reporting and Budgeting
112	Management Grid by		Black and Moutan
113	Marketing concepts in library service		Analysis, Planning, Implementation and Control
114	Margaret Mann is known		Subject of Cataloging
115	Marchand's Stages Of IT Development		Automation Tech. Management (1960-70) Information Resource Management (1970-80) Knowledge Management (Late 1980)
116	Merrill's Code for classifiers was developed	1928	William S. Merrill
117	Michael Stern Hart, who invented	1971	E-Book
118	Million Bank Project was		Carnegie Mellon University
119	Miniature Book is a		Very Small Book
120	Mnemonics for		"Aid To Memory"
121	Mobile Digital Library		C-DAC
122	NACLIN is sponsored by		DELNET
123	Natural Science, Physical Science, and Social Science are		Loose Assemblage
124	Nest Co-Founder Tony Fadell is		Father of the IPOD

125	Non-Programmed type of decisions		Top Level Management
126	Oldest Indian Library Science Journal		Library Miscellany
127	One of the system the optical method is used		Peek-A-Boo System
128	Online search information registration and inquiry system was		IFLA
129	Organization of Knowledge in libraries and subject approach to		H.E. Bliss
130	Organizational Structure is		Span of Control
131	Outdated and seldom used books are		Weeding Out
132	Para linguistics is a		Kind of Complementary Language
133	Pascal Adding Machine was invented	1642	
134	Patron Saint Of Libraries In America, Andrew Carnegie Donated 2 Million Pounds for		Development of library building
135	Periodical Ordering Work includes		Renewal of ordering, New Ordering
136	PERT was developed	1950	U.S. Navy's Polaris Project
137	Phoenix Schedules are		DDC
138	Photo Charging		Ralph R. Shaw ,USA
139	Pigeon Hold Rack is		Periodical Display Rack
140	Plotter is used for		Printing Drawing and Graphs
141	Pool Index To Periodical Literature was		William Frederick
142	POSDCORB		Luther Gulick, Lib. Administration
143	Post coordinate indexes created by		Synonymous terms

144	PPBS Relates to Budgeting	1961	By Rand Corporation
145	PRECIS was developed	1974	Derek Austin
146	Preparation, Service and assimilation by		User Education
147	Principles of is concerned with		Re-Classification
148	Proxemics refers to		The Use of Interpersonal Space
149	RAK is		A Cataloging Code
150	Recall and Precision have been studied		Lancaster
151	SDI Rangnathan coined term		SPEED = S = System, P= Pinpoint Second Law E= Exhaustive Third Law, E= Expeditious Forth Law D= Document
152	Redundancy of information/ Publication means		Unnecessary and should be eliminated
153	Responsible to providing ISSN in India		NISCAIR
154	Ribbon arrangement is associated with		Shelving of books
155	RIC stands for		Rider's International Classification
156	Routing Slip is		Used to circulate periodicals
157	RSS feed is a tool of		Web 2.0
158	Scientific Method can be		Applied for research in all subjects
159	SCIRUS search engine is	2014	Scientific information
160	SDI	1958	H.P Luhn
161	Search Strategy by		W.A. Katz
162	Sheets before and after text of a		End Papers

	book is		
163	Size to size reproduction of documents called		Facsimile
164	Span of Control		The Number of Subordinate to be supervised
165	Standard Size of catalogue card is		12.5 X 7.5cms / 125 Mm X 75 Mm
166	Structural elements to streamline organizational work is known		Strategic Planning
167	SWOT analysis developed		Albert Humphrey
168	Symposium		conference to discuss a particular subject
169	System Theory is developed		Wan Bertalanffy
170	Technical Section two functions		Classification and Ca taloguing
171	Technical Service Coined By		M.F. Tube
172	Term Exponential Growth is referred to		Geometrical Progression
173	Term is "The Practice of Management"	1951	Peter Drucker
174	The 'Quality Circles' organization used		Management Control
175	The "260 Tag" is MARC format publication		Library of Congress
176	The "Grey Literature" means		Internet reports not published as documents
177	The "Roger Payne" was famous		Book Binder
178	The "Task and bonus" system by		Henry Gantt
179	The Concept "Sought Links' is		Chain Indexing
180	The Concept "Disease" is		Energy
181	The Dewey Decimal Classification divides human knowledge		10 Basic Categories
182	The Disadvantage of		Bureaucratic mode is conflict and groupies
183	The Electronic Library is		A Journal name

184	The FID/CA committee on classification theory was found	1950	
185	The First Device to employ concepts similar to a computer war		ABACUS
186	The First stage of binding process known		Collation/ Checking pagination
187	The FRBR final report was first published in print	1998	K.G. Saur , UBCIM Publications
188	The French Term Informatique coined	1962	Philippe Dreyfus
189	The Hectographic process is		Spirit duplicating method
190	The Idea of Thesaurofacet was		Jean Aitchison
191	The ISO 3297 deal with		ISSN
192	The Library Wants to new arrival by display		CAS
193	The Main Entry of classified catalogue code is		Prepared to meet the subject approach
194	The Pioneer of open access system in British Libraries	1932	James Duff Brown
195	The Principle of 'Context Dependency' is associated with		PRECIS
196	The Professorship in library science for the first time was created	1886	Goming University
197	The Quotation where is the wisdom, we have lost the knowledge stated by		T.S. Eliot
198	The Term External Criticism is relived		Historical Method
199	The Relationship term "Ship" and boat" is		Semantic Relation
200	The Title 'Treatment of Lung Disease" is an example of		Compound Subject
201	The concept of "Trinity in Library"		S. R. Rangnathan
202	There are four scales used for		Nominal, Ordinal, Interval and Ratio

			Data
203	Thesaurus terms		Broader Terms(Bt), Narrower Terms(Nt) Related Terms(Rt) and Use For
204	Three Level of Management		Top, Middle, Operational
205	TQM (Total Quality Management) is		Helping employees in an organiz.
206	TRAILS is the document storage system SENDOC		T= Tread Literature, R= Report Literature, A= Area Literature, I= Institutional Literature, L= Library Literature, S= Sundry Literature
207	Translation Service is a feature of		Special Libraries
208	Tree of porphyry is		Schematic Representation of Dichotomy
209	Two is a library management software for small libraries library solution		Baily Solution UK And Follet
210	UBD New Books Bulletin (Monthly)		Universal Book Distributors, Pvt. Ltd, New Delhi
211	UDC common auxiliary of point of view as		Represented by 00
212	UGC of Great Britain	1919	
213	Unity of Commands Means		All Power to one person
214	User Studies in social sciences was		Kuhn
215	Web Browser		Netscape, Mozilla, Opera, MS Internet Explorer, Chrome and Safari

216	What is The Another Name of canon of sought heading		Canon of Recall Value
217	What is EMCO Index		The Computer Produced Expert Medica Index
218	Wheat Load educational exchange programmed	1951	
219	Who Quoted "Library is a people's university"		Canon Cody
220	Who Said "Library is the heart of university"		Charles W. Eliot
221	Workshop		A Series of educational & work sessions
222	Zato Coding was invented by		Calvin Moore's
223	Zero-Based Budgeting (ZBB)	1970	Peter Phyrr

3
Library Services And Information Sources

NATIONAL BIBLIOGRAPHY/ SEARCH SERVICES

S. N.	Bibliographies	Publishers	Places	Years
1	English Bibliography	Cambridge University Press	UK	1546
2	La Librarian	Danny	Italy	1550
3	Bibliotheca Universalis	Kourlad Genser	French	1584
4	BNB (Weekly)	British Library	UK	1950
5	INB (Monthly)	Central Ref. Library, Calcutta	India	1957
6	ESA-IRS	European Space Agency	Italy	1975
7	DIALOG	Polo Alto	California	1972
8	SDC/Orbit	Sautu Monica	California	1972
9	BRS	Asso. of College and Research Libraries	New York	1976
10	BLAISE	British Library	UK	1977

S. R. RANGNATHAN CATEGORIZED INFORMATION SOURCES

S. No.	Information Sources	Examples
1	Conventional	Books, Periodicals, Maps, Atlases, etc.
2	Neo-conventional	Standards, Specifications, Data and the Like, etc.
3	Non-conventional	Microcopy, Audio, Visual, and Audio-Visual Documents, etc.

4	Micro-documents	Instrument Technology, Photography, Radar, and Various other elements.

SIMPLE DUBLIN CORE METADATA ELEMENT SET

S. N.	17 Element Sets
1	Title, creator, subject, description, publisher, Contributor
2	date , type, format, identifier, source, language
3	Relation, coverage, rights, audience, right holder

H. W. HANSON CATEGORIZED INFORMATION SOURCES (TWO TYPES)

Documentary
Books- Treatises, Monographs, Textbooks, Reference Books. Manuscripts • Periodicals • Patents • Standards • Theses • Conference Documents • Souvenirs • Festschriften • Reports (technical, administrative, trip) • Articles (popular, technical, research) • Globes • Diaries • Letters • Office Files • CD-ROM Recordings • Video Recordings • Databases • Computer Files • Laboratory Notebooks.
Non- Documentary
Humans - information Professionals • Consultants • Experts • Resource Persons • Extension Workers • Representatives of Firms • Technological Gatekeepers • invisible College • Common Men, etc.
Organisations- international Agencies • Government Ministries and Departments • Research and Development Organisations • Academic institutions • Societies • Publishing Houses • Press • Broadcasting Houses • Libraries and information Centres • Museums • Archives • Exhibitions • Trade Fairs • Database Vendors • information Analysis Centres • Referral Centres, etc.
World Wide Web-(Print)- Books • Periodicals • Patents • Standards • Conference Documents • Souvenirs • Festschriften • Reports (technical, administrative, trip) • Articles (popular, technical, research). (Non-Print)- Manuscripts (typed or hand-written) • Theses • Project Reports (typed) • Diaries • Letters • Office Files • Laboratory Notebooks • Microforms • CD Recordings • Video Recordings • Databases • Computer Files • E-publications etc.

BIBLIOGRAPHIC FORMAT AND STANDARDS

S. N.	Format	Explanation
1	BIBCO	Bibliographic Coded- Monographs
2	CONSER	Serial bibliography Record- Serial
3	NACO	Name Authority Coded- Name
4	SACO	Subject Authority Coded-Library Information Science

DENIS GROGAN CATEGORIZED INFORMATION SOURCES

S. No.	Information Sources	Examples
1	Primary	Periodicals (solely devoted to report original work) • Research Reports • Conference Proceedings • Reports of Scientific Expeditions • Official Publications • Patents • Standards • Trade Literature • Theses and Dissertations • Laboratory Notebooks • Diaries • Memoranda • internal Research Reports • Minutes of Meetings • Company Files • Correspondence • Personal Files, etc.
2	Secondary	• Periodicals (non-primary) – Abstracting Services – indexing Services – Reviews of Progress • Reference Books, e.g., – Encyclopedias – Dictionaries – Handbooks – Tables – Formularies • Treatises • Monographs, and • Textbooks
3	Tertiary sources	• Yearbooks • Directories • Bibliographies (List of Books, Location Lists of Periodicals, Lists of indexing and Abstracting Services) • Guides to 'The Literature' • Lists of Research in Progress • Guides to Sources of information • Guides to Libraries • Guides to Organizations.

Reference Cited In Bibliography Formats		
S. N.	Formats	Explains
1	Ibid	Same reference cited immediately above
2	Loc. cit.	The same place cited
3	Op. cit	Previously cited
4	Vide	See

INTERNATIONAL/ NATIONAL INFORMATION DOCUMENTATIONS CENTRE / ORGANIZATIONS

S. N.	Organizations	Place/ Counties	Years
1	Patent information System (PIS)	Nagpur, India	1980
2	International Council of Scientific Union (ICSU)	Brussels, Belgium	1931
3	Food and Agriculture Organization (FAO)	Rome, Italy	1938
4	University Grand Commission (UGC)	New Delhi, India	1953
5	International Atomic Energy Agency (IAEA)	Viena, Austria	1957
6	Defence Research & Develop. Organization (DRDO)	New Delhi, India	1958
7	Documentation Research & Training Center (DRTC)	Bangalore, India	1962
8	World intellectual Property Organization (WIPO)	Geneva, Switzerland	1967
9	Bhabha Automic Research Center (BARC)	Mumbai, India	1967
10	international Nuclear information System (INIS)	Viena, Austria	1970
11	Agricultural information System of FAO (AGRIS)	Rome, Italy	1975
12	Indian National Scientific Documentation Center (INSDOC)	New Delhi, India	1952
13	Defence Scientific Documentation Center (DESIDOC)	New Delhi, India	1958
14	National Social Science	New Delhi, India	1969

	Documentation Center (NASSDOC)		
15	Small Scale Enterprise National Documental Center (SENDOC)	Hyderabad, India	1971
16	National information Center (NIC)	New Delhi, India	1975
17	National information System for Science and Technology (NISSAT)	Calcutta, India	1977

INFLIBNET, 1991 (AHMADABAD)

S. N.	Activities	Programs
1	E-Consortium	UGC-INFONET DLC-2002
2		N-LIST Program-2010 (National Library and Information Services Infrastructure for Scholarly Content)
3	E-PG Pathshala	2014
4	IndCat Union Database	1996
	Open Access Initiative	INFOPORT-2010
		IR@ INFONET
		OJAS-2018
		Shodhgang-2009
		ShodhGangotri-2009
	Research Project	
	SOUL	2000
	VIDWAN Database	2014
	INDEST-AICTE Consortium-2013	IIT Delhi
		E-Shodh Sindhu Consortium-2012

BIBLIOGRAPHY MANUAL OF STYLES

S. N.	Bibliographies	Founders	Editions	Years
1	Chicago Manual of Style (1906)	University of Chicago Press	17 Ed.	2017
2	APA (1929)	American Psychiatric Ass ociation	7 Ed.	2019
3	Turabian (1937)	University of Chicago Press	9 Ed.	2018
4	MLA (1985)	Modern Languag. Asso. of America	8 Ed.	2019

THESAURUS AND PUBLISHERS

S. N.	Thesaurus	Publishers	Places	Years
1	Root Thesaurus	BSI	UK	
2	Spines Thesaurus	UNESCO	Paris, France	
3	INSPEC Thesaurus	inst. of Electrical Engineers	UK	
4	Thesaurus of Engineering and scientific Terms	Engineers Joint Council	USA	1967
5	Information retrieval thesaurus of education terms	Case Western Reserve University		1968
6	Thesaurus Facet	English Electric Co.	UK	1969
7	OECD Macro Thesaurus	int. Labour organization	Geneva	1972
8	INIS Thesaurus	IAEA	Vienna	1973

ENCYCLOPEDIAS

S. N.	Encyclopedias	Publishers/ Places	Years
1	Ency. of Religion and Ethics	Edinburgh	1908
2	The new book of Knowledge	Canada	1966
3	International Ency. of Social Science	New York	1967
4	Ency. of Library and information sc	New York	1968
5	New Encyclopedia Britannica	Chicago	1974
6	Encyclopedia Indica	New Delhi	1975

7	Encyclopedia Americana-30 Vol.	New York	1976
8	Collier Encyclopedia	New York	1976
9	Marathi Vishwakosh	Mumbai	1976
10	Mc-Graw Hill Ency. of Science & Technology	New York	1977

ABSTRACTING SERVICES

S. N.	Services	Publishers	Places	Years
1	Engineering index	Association Of Engineering Societies	New York	1884
2	Physics Abstract	institute Of Electrical Engineers	London	1898
3	Chemical Abstract	American Chemical Society	Easton Philadelphia	1907
4	Biological Abstract	American Chemical Society	Easton Philadelphia	1926
5	Psychological Abstract	American Psychological Publication	Washington	1927
6	Bulletin Signaletique	Centre National De La Recherche Scientifigue	Paris	1940
7	Excerpt Medica	Excerpt Medica Fondation	Amsterdam	1947
8	Library and Information Science Abstract	Library Association	Landon	1950
9	Sociological Abstract		New York	1952
10	Economic Abstract	Martinus Nijhoff	The Hague	1953
11	Indian Science Abstract	INSDOC	New Delhi	1965
12	Information Science Abstract	Documentation Abstracts	New Delhi	1966
13	Indian Library Science Abstract	IASLIC	Calcutta	1967

14	COMPuterized ENgineering index	(COMPENDEX) EngineeringVillage.com	Brazil	1995
15	Compendex abstracts	Elsevier	Brazil	1998

NATIONAL INFORMATION SYSTEMS FOR SCIENCE AND TECHNOLOGY-CALCUTTA, 1977

S. N.	Sectors systems	Works	Places
1	NICLAI	Leather Technology	Chennai
2	NICFOS	Food Technology	Mysore
3	NICMAP	Machine tools and Products	Bangalore
4	NICDAP	Drug and Pharmaceuticals	Lukhnow
5	NICTAS	Textiles and Allied Subjects	Ahmadabad
6	NICHEM	Chemicals NCL	Pune
7	NICAS	Glass and Ceramics	Culcutta
8	NICRYS	Crystallography	Madras
9	NCB	Bibliometrics, NISCAR	Delhi
10	CDROM	National Aero Space	Bangalore

TYPES OF BIBLIOGRAPHY

S. N.	Types	Means
1	Analytical Bibliography	Analytical or critical bibliography therefore rests to a large extent upon imperfection in the production process.
2	Descriptive Bibliography	Descriptive bibliography is the application of analytical bibliography to the external form of the book.
3	Textual Bibliography	It is an application of analytical bibliography to the contexts of books.
4	Historical Bibliography	The study of books "as object of art" may be termed a historical bibliography.
5	Systematic Bibliography	Systematic bibliography is nothing but the listing of books and other reading materials.

ACCORDING TO SOURCE DIVIDED THE BIBLIOGRAPHY

S. N.	A- primary	Means
1	General or Universal Bibliography	It attempts to include books published in every country and age and on all subject.
2	Incunabula Bibliography	This type of bibliography lists the early printed material upto 15th century.
3	Bibliography of anonymous and pseudonymous works	The bibliographies are arranged alphabetically by title with notes of author, details of publication.
4	Trade bibliographies	These types of bibliographies are brought out by large publishing firms engaged in book production or trade.
5	National bibliography	It is a comprehensive, almost complete record of both written and printed output in a given country.

S. N.	B- secondary	Means
1	Subject Bibliography	A subject bibliography is a comprehensive list of all books, articles, pamphlets and other analytical materials.
2	Author Bibliography	An author bibliography is the list of writing by an author together with the works on him by others.
3	Personal Bibliography	A personal bibliography is a list of writings by others on the different aspects of the life of a great man together.
4	Bibliophilic Bibliography	A bibliography that records old and rare books, first editions of celebrated authors is known as bibliophilic bibliography.
5	Selective Bibliography (Elective)	This kind of bibliography is concerned with the listing of only selected and the best books.

6	Unit Bibliography	The every literary work by every author does not deserve a unit bibliography.
7	Bibliography of Bibliographies (Bibliographic Index)	The various subject fields have multiplied now a day the compilation of this kind of bibliography has become imperative.

THE SECTIONS OF THE MAIN ENTRY AS CLASSIFIED CATALOGUE CODE

S. N.	Sections	Explains
1	Leading Section	Call number of the document
2	Heading Section	Entry element
3	Title Section	Title, subtitle
4	Note Section	The series
5	Accession Number	1562
6	Tracing	The back of main entry card

PROCESSING OF BOOKS IN CATALOGUING

S.N.	Process	Explains
1	Stamping	It is necessary to put a library stamp on lower half of the title page, bottom of the last page of text, bottom of the last page of the volume, and the secret page.
2	Tagging	Paste a tag (spine label) on the back of the volume, after removing the jacket, if any. It should be fixed one inch above the bottom of the spine of the volume.
3	Date Labelling	A date label or slip should be pasted on the first page after the cover. It should be fixed symmetrically and pasting should be done only along the top edge.
4	Book Pocket Fixing	Near the right hand bottom corner of the inside of the front cover of the book, the pocket should be fixed.
5	Book Card	One printed book card of 5X 3 cm size is put in the book pocket of each book.
6	Fixing	Ownership slip is generally pasted on the inner

	Ownership Slip	side of the front cover at left hand top most corners.
7	Entering Call Number	The call number should be written in pencil at the back of the title page and also on the secret page to be decided by the library.
8	Entering Accession Number	Accession number is to be added on the date label, book card and to the written near the book pocket.
9	Filling Book Card	Author, title, edition and year of publication are written on the book card.
10	Checking	All the call numbers and catalogue entries must be carefully checked. Any mistakes found must be corrected.
11	Filling of Cards	The catalogue cards should be taken out from the books. From the main cards, a list of latest additions can be prepared.

THE PROMINENT E-MAIL REFERENCE SERVICES

S. N.	Service	Organisation	Subject	Payment
1	Askme	Askme.com	All	Free
2	Allexperts	Allexperts.com	All	Free
3	Inforocket	Inforocket.com	All	Free-based
4	Askauntienolo	Nolo.com	Law	Free
5	Find/svp	Findsvp.com	Business	Free-based
6	Professional city	Professionalcity.com	Law	Free-based

THE REAL TIME DIGITAL REFERENCE SERVICES

S. N.	Services	S. N.	Services
1	Ask a question	9	Click for Live Help
2	Ask Now	10	E-Gateway
3	Ask the Librarian	11	Infochat
4	Ask-A- Librarian	12	Librarians Online
5	Chat Reference Assistance	13	Library Chat
6	Chat with A Librarian	14	Need Help? Ask A Librarian
7	Ask Us Now	15	Virtual Reference Desk
8	Chat with Us	16	Refchat

WEB DIRECTORIES

S. N.	Process	Explains
1	Yahoo! (*http://in.dir.yahoo.com/*)	Yahoo! aims to be the biggest Internet directories, with a high level of coverage and popular appeal as high priorities. It is an excellent site for finding topics that appeal to the general public. Currently, a search in Yahoo is being passed to AltaVista. However, people can still use its directory.
2	Open Directory Project (*http://dmoz.org/*)	Open Directory lists scholarly and popular websites. The Open Directory Project, also known as Directory Mozilla (DMOZ), relies on a volunteer work force of editors who, by selecting, classifying and cataloguing resources, are trying to build the largest library on the Internet. The raw open-source directory is used by Google, Netscape Search, AOL Search, Lycos, HotBot, and DirectHit.
3	BUBL Link (*http://bubl.ac.uk/*)	BUBL Link uses the Dewey Decimal Classification system as the primary organization structure for its catalogue of Internet resources. It carefully selected and accurately catalogued many LIS resources. It was developed by Centre for Digital Library Research, Department of Computer and Information Sciences, University of Strathclyde, Livingstone Tower, 26 Richmond Street, Glasgow G1 1XH, Scotland.
4	About.com	At About.com (*http://www.about.com/*) you'll find a directory with a twist. Each topic area has an assigned "Guide" responsible for writing articles and organizing links on the topic.

FUNCTIONAL BLOCK OF UNIVERSAL MACHINE READABLE CATALOGUE (UNIMARC)

Block	Field tag	Data Type	Example
0	000-099	Identification Block	Contains numbers that identify the record. Eg. 010 International Standard Book Number.
1	100-199	Coded Information Block	Contains fixed length data element describing various aspect of the record or data. Eg. 101 Language of the work
2	200-299	Heading Block	Contains the authority, reference or general explanatory heading for which records have been created. Eg. 205 Edition statements.
3	300-399	Information Note Block	Contains note, intended for public display that explain the relationship between the record heading and other heading.
4	400-499	See Reference Tracing Block	Contains variant heading from which a reference is to be made to see the heading of the record. Eg. 452 Edition in a different medium.
5	500-599	See Also Reference Tracing Block	Contains related uniform heading from which a reference is to be made to see also the heading of the record. Eg. 516 Spine title.
6	600-699	Classification Number Block	Contains classification number that are related to the heading of the record. Eg. 676 Dewey Decimal Classification.
7	700-799	Linking Heading Block	Contains a form of the record heading in another language and links to another record in which that form is the heading. Eg. 700 Personal name
8	800-	Source	Contains the source of the record and

	899	Information Block	catalogues notes. Eg. 801 Originating Source
9	900-999	National use Block	Contains data local to the originator of the record.

STRATEGIES IN LIBRARIAN NEEDS TO ESTABLISHING A REFERENCE AND INFORMATION SERVICE

S.N.	Steps	Explains
1	Determining Aims and Objectives of the Library	The kind of reference service being provided would vary from library to library.
2	Staffing	Library and information science professionals should be appointed to look after the on-demand reference and information service.
3	Facilities Organization	In addition to an extensive research/reading room, there is also the need of a multimedia room equipped with high-speed computers.
4	Building Reference Collection	The maintenance of the print reference collections including dictionaries, directories, and encyclopedia is a must for any kind of reference service.
5	Gathering Knowledge of the Subject	The librarian should have a sound knowledge about all the reference collections in his library. He should also know about the search engine, subject directories and so on.
6	Marketing/Visibility	The library reference services should be marketed extensively to get the attention of the library users.
7	Origin of the Query	Queries to the Reference Librarian can be made by the library user himself physically, by post, through phone calls, email, online chat, and so on.
8	Reference Interview	A user will feel the need for information.
9	Initiating the Search	The Reference Librarian should pick

		up the keywords to search in bibliographies, indexes, online databases, subject search engines and so on.
10	Solving the Query	The reference librarian finds out and provides the answer to a specific question raised by the library user.
11	Ethics and the Provision of High Quality Service	The library users have different psychological temperaments, some are meek and inert, and some have a superiority complex.
12	Assimilation	In the reference service experience is the most important thing.
13	Sharing Experience & Others	A reference librarian should try to share his experience with his colleagues in the reference section.
14	Continuing Education of Reference Librarians	The reference librarian should be regularly sent for training.

TYPES OF DATABASE

S.N.	Database	Means
1	Bibliographic	Bibliographic databases the data stored comprise input of bibliographical details of a document for identification, storage and retrieval purposes.
1-A	Internal database and associated services	The internal bibliographic databases are those created by libraries.
1-B	External database and associated services	External bibliographic databases comprise online catalogues such as SCISEARCH.
2	Numerical Databases	It contains numeric or statistical or survey type data of information to give answer of numeric queries.
3	Full Text Database	Full text databases contain the full text of a publication, i. e. provide relevant information directly.

4	Factual Database	Factual database contains directory type data.
5	Research in Progress Database	It contains description of research in progress.

DEVELOPING LIBRARY NETWORK-1991

S.N.	Functions and Activities	Explains
1	Resource Sharing	DELNET saved foreign exchange worth Rs. 10 million by rationalizing subscriptions to foreign periodicals.
2	Online Databases	DELNET has around twenty databases available online for their users which include Union Catalogue of Books.
3	DDS	DELNET members can place their inter-library loan requests through their ILL online facility.
4	Development of Software	DELNET provided CDS/ISIS software for storage and retrieval purpose, developed by UNESCO through NISSAT, but presently is software DELSIS, DELDOS and DEL-WINDOWS for creating MARC records.
5	Standardization	A standardization committee of DELNET has been meeting from time to time.
6	Seminars, Conferences, Workshops and Training	DELNET also organizes national workshops, seminars and meets on library networking from time to time and National Annual convention on Library and Information Networking (NACLIN) regularly.
7	Publications	DELNET has been publishing a newsletter (1994) in order to increase awareness about library networking in India and publishes NACLIN Proceedings, Director's Report, etc.
8	Mailing Lists and	DELNET has created a Listserv service

	Forum	called DEL-LISTSERV to provide the current awareness service and maintains other Listserv service such as Net-happenings, Med-clips, IFLA, LIBJOBS, etc.
9	Others	DELNET System for Information Services (DELSIS) is library network software developed by DELNET. DEL SEARCH is a database access mechanism by DELNET.

MARKETING OF PRODUCT AND SERVICES

S.N.	Marketing	Resources
1	Why of Marketing-Needs	Maximum Use of Library Resources.
		Justifiable Expansion Programme.
		For Self Survival.
		Generating Funds.
2	What is Marketing-Products	Print Media: Books, Journals, Bibliographies, and Directories etc.
		Electronic Information Product and Services: Diskette, Floppies etc.
		Online Information Product and Services: Online journal, networking products etc.
		Other Services: Xeroxing, translation services.
3	How of Marketing	A market research is essential to determine user needs, available services, operation and cost, longevity of demand etc.
		Market segmentation is the segmentation of the clientele/ users on the basis of individual differences and group similarities.
		In the development of the product, its periodicity, content aspect, coverage/ scope, pricing.
		Price generally depends on objectives

		of the product, nature of cost involved, level of demand of the product etc.
4	Promotion	Propaganda through the newspaper, radio, television can be done in the public community.
		On the occasion of fair, festival, book fair and other programmes in the nearest area of the libraries, exhibitions of marketing services.
		Study circles among the users of the libraries can also be organized to marketing the information service.
		Mobile libraries are a great way to reach the unreached.
		The library services can also be marketed through CAS/SDI services.
5	Distribution	Inter Personnel Delivery: Products that are personally delivered.
		Group Personnel Delivery: Product delivered at meeting, conference, seminar, demonstration etc.
		Mass Media: Through newspaper, professional journals, magazines etc.
		Broadcasting: Through radio, television etc.
		Information Technology: Telephone, Computer, Email.
6	Evaluation	A continuous built in evaluation procedure should be followed to assess the capabilities and weakness of the product/service, distribution channel etc.
7	Barriers of Marketing	Structural: Staff coming into the contact with users is not information professionals; hence there is no staff to think from the user point or side.
		Systematic: Library and information system don't seem to allow the client or client point of view inside the

		system.
		Attitudinal: Libraries remains happy with satisfying a limited user that too when asked for.
		Environment: The culture still believes in that information should be free.

DIGITAL MEDIA PRESERVATION AND CONSERVATION TECHNIQUES

S.N.	Two Terminologies	
1	1- Digital curation is the selection, preservation, maintenance, collection and archiving of digital assets.	2- Digital obsolescence is a situation where a digital resource is no longer readable because the physical media.
2	**Digital Media- Techniques**	
2.1	Avoiding Physical Deterioration of Media- The media on which digital contents are stored are more vulnerable to deterioration and catastrophic loss than some analog media such as paper.	
2.2	Refreshing-Refreshing is the task of transferring contents between two types of the same storage medium.	
2.3	Replication-Replication is the process of creating multiple copies of the digital document and keeping them in multiple locations.	
2.4	Bit-stream Copying- Backing up data refers to the process of making an exact duplicate of the original digital object.	
2.5	Migration-The biggest problem to the digital media preservation is the storage format evaluation and its obsolescence.	
2.6	Emulation-Emulation uses emulator, a special kind of software that translates code and instructions from one computing environment.	
2.7	Metadata Attachment-Metadata is data on a digital file that includes information on creation, access rights, restrictions, preservation history, and management.	
2.8	Analogue Backups-It is the process of the conversion of digital objects into analogue format.	
2.9	Technology Preservation- It deals with the preservation of the technology in which the digital information was created and	

	maintained. It deals with the issues of preserving the technology.
2.10	Digital Archaeology- Digital archaeology includes methods and procedures to rescue the content from damaged media, hardware or software environments.

LIBRARY SERVICES AND SOURCES TERMS

S. N.	Library terms	Years	Explains
1	A questionnaire is		flexible
2	Abstracting Service Provides		Bibliographic Description and Abstracts of Article
3	Analytical Bibliography Is		The Facts And Data Concerning A Publication
4	APS is		Full-Text E-Resources
5	Article Published in Research Journal		Primary Sources
6	Best Books to the maximum readers at the least cost	1876	Melvil Dewey
7	Bibliographic database service (BIOSIS) -	1926	Philadelphia, United States
8	Bibliographies and Abstracts –Example		information Consolidation
9	Book Selection Committee Is		Standing Committee
10	Books lost from the library are known		Charging and discharging
11	Browne Charging System Started	1895	
12	Budget Which Mainly Covers Items of Current Revenue and Expenditure is		Capital Budget
13	CAS is		current Awareness Services
14	CAS is Defined		Current information
15	Cataloging in Publication	1971	Library of Congress
16	CERA is a consortia for		Agriculture Sciences

			Literanture
17	Citation Generators Are		Online Tools Which Facilitate The Creation Of Works
18	Collection of Maps, Tables, Charts		Atlas
19	Compton Year Book Covered		Outstanding Events
20	Concept of Reference Service given by		Samuel S Green
21	Conference proceedings are		Primary documents
22	Council of Scientific and Industrial Research (CSIR)	1942	Government of India
23	COURTNIC	1991	N. Delhi, Government of India
24	Cover to Cover Translation is		Current Awareness Services
25	Cumulative Book index	1898	H. W. Wilson, USA
26	Data India (Weekly) by	1963	Press institute of india
27	DDC classification scheme Pub.	1876	1st Journal of the librarianship
28	Defence Research and Development Organization (DRDO)	1958	Ministry Of Defence, Government of India
29	DEL-PLUS software was designed		DELNET.
30	Diazo Process is used for Making Copies of		Micro Document
31	Dictionary of Anonymous and Pseudonymous Literature		S. Halkett & J. Laing
32	Department of Science & Technology (DST)	1971	Ministry of Science and Technology in India
33	Demand and Supply Theory of Books		Mc Colvin Moors
34	Document Supply Center of the British Library		Lending Division

	known as		
35	E.C. Richardson defined notation as		short and sign
36	E-Documents		Cassettes, CD-ROMS, Etc.
37	Education and Research Network in India provided first e-mail service in	1986	
38	Electrically Operated Book Charging System	1932	
39	Endnote is a product of		Thomson Reuters Company
40	Facts On File (Weekly List)		NEWYORK
41	Father Of Bibliography		Conrad Gesner
42	Financial Support to Libraries are Two Types		Recurring and Non-Recuing / Endowments
43	First Editor of "Modern Librarian"		F. Monbrary Volte
44	First PhD in Lib & inf. Science in India	1957	D.B. Krishna Rao. Delhi university
45	First Time Efforts For The Development of Libraries in India		S.R. Rangnathan
46	Fishery Survey of India		Mumbai
47	Four entity of FRBR model are		Work, Expression, Manifestation, Item
48	Free Software Movement		Richard Stallman
49	Fritz Matchup introduced the concept		'Knowledge Industry'
50	Gazetteer (Ministry of Home Affairs) N. Delhi	1950	Information of A Particular Place
51	Grogan by documents three types		Primary, Secondary and Tertiary
52	Guide Book		Historical Monuments of Delhi
53	Guinness Book Of World Records		NEWYORK

54	Herbert Simon define Authority as		"power to make decision and audience to other"
55	Honored With 'Nobel Prize' For		Henri La Fontaine
56	Historical Bibliography		The Book Production I.e.-Printing Binding , Paper Making, Illustrating And Publishing
57	How Many Columns are Accession Register		14 Columns, Size 16" X 13"
58	ILA 60 Year Diamond Jubilee	2015	Chandigarh
59	Impact of User Education On Library Use Patterns" 'Library Use'		An Dependent Variable
60	In CC LED stands for		Latest Effective Decade
61	Incunabula Means		The Book Printed Before 1501 A.D.
62	India Who's Who by		INFA Publication, Delhi
63	India: A Reference Annual		Year Book
64	Indian Books in Print		New Delhi
65	Indian Council of Agricultural Research (ICAR)	1936	Deptt. of Agricultural Research and Education, N. Delhi-India
66	Indian Council of Historical Research (ICHR)	1971	Government of India
67	Indian Council of Medical Research (ICMR)	1969	Government of India
68	Indian Council of Philosophical Research (ICPR)	1981	Government of India
69	Indian Council of Social Science Research (ICSSR)	1969	Government of India
70	Indian Standards institution (1955) Known	1987	Bureau of Indian Standards
71	INFLIBNET document delivery centers are		University of Hyderabad Library & Lukhnow University Library

72	Information Gatekeepers come under		Documentary sources
73	Information Science By Wesig	1993	Postmodern Science
74	Information Society (American Society for information Science)	1986	Brascom
75	Institute for Studies in industrial Development-ISID is		E-Bibliographic database
76	International Book Year celebrated	1972	UNESCO
77	International Labour organization (ILO)	1919	American Federation of Labour in United States
78	Introduction to Librarianship is		J.K. Gate
79	Introduction to Reference Source		W.A. Katz
80	J.D. Brown in famous for his		One-Place Theory
81	Journals of Elsevier Science all user	2012	NISCAIR, New Delhi (Science Direct)
82	Kardex used		maintain a visible record of periodical in library
83	Keesings Record Of World Events (Monthly)		London
84	Kurt Sanford CEO, of Pro Quest related to		Dissertation Abstracts International
85	LA is the Library Association	1877	Great Britain
86	LAMP Stands For		Linux Apache, Mysql, Perl
87	Library Budget of A University is		Executive Counseling
88	Library Budget Takes Items of Expenditure For Libraries		Allocation of Funds
89	Library Herald (Quarterly)	1958	Delhi Library Asso. (Krishan Kumar)

90	Library literature is		tertiary source
91	Linedex system used for		displaying the periodicals holding
92	List of Books in Print Or For Sale By		Trade Bibliography
93	LIS-Forum is(e-mail based discussio.. forum for Library and information professionals)	1995	NCSI, indian institute of Science, Bangalore
94	Management by Objectives	1954	Peter F. Drucker
95	Manual of Library Economy is		J.D. Brown
96	MARC as a pilot project was LC	1966	260 tag is MARC Format marks
97	MeSH is Controlled Vocabulary tool	1964	MEDLARS
98	Mobile Library is		Extension Service
99	Modular Construction Is		Model Building
100	National Bibliography	1957	Particular Nation
101	New Encyclop. Britannica-Ready References		Propaedia
102	New York Charging System		John Cotton Dana
103	Non-Parametric Test are		U-Test, Kruskal-Wallis Test, Run-Test, T-Test, Null Hypothesis, F-Test
104	Non-Recuing Expenses are		Capital Expenses-Building, Furniture and Fittings, Computer Etc.
105	Old and Fragile Book Preserved By		Microfilming, Re-Binding, Digesting
106	Online Europa Year Book	1985	
107	Ontology is		Classification of internet based documents
108	Open Access System in British Libraries		James Duff Brown
109	Peer Review is		Pre-Publication Articles Scrutiny
110	Physical condition of books		Property maintained

	should be		Conservation
111	Principle of Maximum Aggregate Benefit is		Library Service
112	Pwxyz LCC Publishes		Weekly
113	Readers' Guide to Periodical Literature	1901	H. W. Wilson, USA
114	Reading Centre, Story Hours, Exhibition and Reading to Literature are		Extension Service
115	Recurring Funds Used		Other Purposes
116	Reference Service is		Right Reader, Right Book Right, Personal Way-S.R. Rangnathan
117	Reference service of a library processed stages are		Preparation, Service, and Assimilation
118	Reference Sources Covered		Particular information
119	Reference was defined by	1935	James I Wyer
120	Retrospective Search Service		Responsive Service
121	Retrospective search service is		Reference service
122	S.R.Ranganathan Coined Mobile Libraries		Library On Wheels
123	SAARC documentation centre	1985	Bangladesh
124	Samuel Rothstein expanded I Wyer's theory	1960	Characterizing Reference Service As "minimum, 'middling' and 'maximum"
125	Scrutiny of Financial Transactions is		Auditing
126	SDI service demands		'user' profile
127	Secondary Source of information		Indexing and Abstracting Periodicals
128	Selective Dissemination of information (SDI) was	1959	H.P. Luhn of IBM
129	Semantic web are		RDF, Ontology's, URI

130	Service Demands 'User' Profile and Feedback Mechanism	1959	SDI
131	Shelf list is an		Important record of books
132	Specification is		Legal Document
133	Stacks		Storages the various types of documents in a library
134	Statesman Year Book, Annually	1864	Macmillan, (London)
135	Stoner define that		construction and destruction more democratic and less authorities
136	STRN Is For		Technical Report
137	SUPLIS	1992	Boston
138	Term Library 2.0 was first coined		Michael Casey
139	Term Web2.0 was coined		Darcy Divacci
140	The "Quantity Theory of information"	1949	Shannon & Weaver
141	The Association of Research Libraries	1932	
142	The biggest library in the world	1800	Library of Congress
143	The Chi-Square Test Indicates		Non-Parametric Test
144	The 'Conservative, moderate and liberal theories of reference service'	1930	James I Wyer
145	The Dewey Decimal Classification divides human knowledge		10 basic categories
146	The Different Between Expenditure		Zero Based Budgeting
147	The FRBR Final Report was first published in print	1998	K.G. Saur , UBCIM publications
148	The journal of Library and		Interblending and

	information Science is		Document supply
149	The Publisher of " Encyclopedia Of Library and Information Science"		Marcel Dekker
150	The Renardus-Multi/Academic Subject Gateway Service	2002	Europe
151	The Term "Grace Weeks " Is Used		Periodical Section
152	The Word 'Encyclopedia' was first by	1559	Paul Scalich
153	The word information Science first	1956	Chris Hanson, ASLIB-UK
154	The Encyclopedia Britannica-32 Vol.	1768	Scotland. New York – Micro, Macro and Propædia-2012
155	Theory of Book Selection	1925	L. R. Mc-Colvin
156	Thesaurus		Synonymous Terms/ List of Words
157	Thesis		Primary Sources
158	Three Card System By S. R. Rangnathan		Register Card, Check Card, Classified index Card
159	Two Parts of The Annual Report of Library		Descriptive and Statistical
160	Types of Extension Services		Library Websites, Library Orientation, Book Fair and Exhibition
161	Universities Hand Book: India		Association Of Indian Universities, Delhi
162	User education may be provided areas which are		User's awareness, user studies, library orientation, bibliographic instruction
163	V.I.N.I.T.I is center of		RUSSIA
164	W.A. KATZ Used		Phrase Control-Access Directional Type Sources
165	Web-Scale Services- Users to Librarians	2015	Punjab University, Chandigarh
166	What is full text e-		American chemical

	Resource		society
167	Who's Who is		Biographical Source Of Information
168	Who is known as "Biblioclast"		A Destroyer of Book
169	Who publishes Annals of Library Science and documentation INSDOC now	2002	NISCAR
170	Who's Who of Indian Writers by		Sahitya Academy, Delhi
171	Who told that organization is a machine		Wilson and Tauber
172	Word of Learning-Directory (Secondary Source)		Europa Pub., London (UK)
173	Xerography is		Electrostatic
174	Year Book		Annually
175	Zero Based Budget	1970	Peter Phyor
176	ZOTERO Is		Bibliographic Ref. Mangt. System

4

Information Retrieval and Indexing Systems

INDEXING SYSTEM

S.N.	Indexing	Years	Founders	Born
1	Subject indexing	1923	Minnie Earl Sears	1873
2	Automated indexing	1958	H. Ohlman	1893
3	SLIC indexing	1966	J.R. Sharp	1695
4	Zator System	1947	Calvin Moores	1919
5	Selecto System	1980	Anna Cordennie	1893
6	NEPHIS (Nested-Phrase indexing System)	1977	Timothy C. Craven	1960
7	LIPHIS (Linked Phrase indexing System)	1978	Timothy C. Craven	1960
8	Thesaurus indexing	1852	P.M. Rogget	1779
9	Systematic indexing	1911	H.J. Kaiser	1882
10	Chain indexing	1938	Dr. S.R. Rangnathan	1892
11	Relation Analysis	1950	Farradabce	1950
12	Uniterm indexing	1953	Mortimer Taube	1910
13	Key Word indexing	1959	Hans Peter Luhn	1896
14	Citation indexing	1963	J.A. Garfield	1831
15	BTI indexing	1963	T.N. Coates	1975
16	PREserved Context indexing System	1974	Derik Austin	1921
17	Postulate Based Permuted Subject indexing	1964	G. Bhattacharya	1937
18	Compass Indexing (Computer Aided Subject System)	1991	BNB	1950

19	Classarus	1959	G. Bhattacharya	1937
20	Theauro Facet	1969	Jean Aitchinsion	1938

LIBRARY AND INFORMATION SCIENCE IN DATABASES

S. N.	Databases	years	Publisher /year	Org/Places
1	Chemical Index	1860	The American Chemical Society	USA
2	Citation Index	1960	Institute for Scientific Information (ISI)	USA
3	Science Citation Index	1964	ISI, Philadelphia	Eugene Garfield Quarterly, USA
4	Social Sciences Citation Index	1973	(ISI) from Thomson Reuters-2008, USA	The Science Citation Index
5	Humanities Index	1974	H.W. Wilson ; New York	Quarterly
6	Arts & Humanities Search	1975	ISI, Philadelphia, 1960	USA
7	Web of Science	2009	Thomson Reuters (1900)	Citation Index
8	Dissertations Abstracts	1938	University Microfilms International (UMI) / Pro Quest (1938)	Bibliography of American Dissertations
9	ERIC	1986	Institute of Education Sciences of the United States Department of Education (1966)	Digital Library of Education Research and Information
10	INSPEC	1967	Institution of Engineering and Technology, (1967)	Fields of Physics and Computer
11	Library and	1969	Bowker and Saur,	Library and

	Information Science Abstracts (LISA)		Landon (1898)	Information Science
12	Book Inprint (Weekly)	1872	R.R. Bowker, 1868	USA
13	Agricola		U.S. Dept of Agriculture, USA	USA
14	Library, Information Science & Technology Abstracts	1984	H. W. Wilson Company. (1898)	Library and Information Science periodicals
15	Cancer Line		National Library of Medicine	USA
16	CA Search	1957	The American Chemical Society	USA
17	SCI search		ISI, PHILADEPHIA	USA
18	British Book inprint	1874	England	UK
19	Bengal Royal Asiatic Society	1784	Bengal	India
20	Bombay Royal Asiatic Society	1804	Bombay	India
21	India Science Index	1972	Gurgaon	Yearly
22	Index MEDICUS	1960	NLM, USA	Monthly
23	Current Content	1957	ISI, Philadelphia (Now Thomson Scientific)	Weekly
24	Chemical Titles	1960	American Chemical Society	Fortnightly
25	British Technology Index	1962	H.W. Wilson ; New York	Monthly
26	Biological & Agricultural Index	1964	H.W. Wilson ; New York	Monthly
27	Applied Science	1913	H.W. Wilson ; New	Monthly

	and Technology index		York	
28	The Reader Guide to Periodical Literature	1900	H.W. Wilson ; New York	Monthly
29	Index India	1967	Rajasthan University Library	Quarterly
30	Guide to Indian Periodical Literature	1964	Gurgaon	Quarterly
31	Whitaker & Almanac	1868	Reference Book	UK
32	Ulrich international Periodical Directories	1932		
33	Whitaker	1970	New Kensington	UK
34	Pool's index Periodical Literature	1802		
35	Web of Knowledge	2001	ISI/ Thomson Reuters	USA
36	H-INDEX	2005		
37	G- INDEX	2006		
38	EBSCO	1944		USA
39	Reed Elsevier, PLC	2017	Academic Libraries	USA
40	Journal Impact Factor	1975		
41	Publisher (Weekly)	1872	R.R. Bowker	USA
42	Book imprint (Annualy)	1948	R.R. Bowker	USA
43	Indian book inprint	1957	Central Reference Library	Calcutta

SOCIETY OF COLLEGE, NATIONAL AND UNIVERSITY LIBRARY, SCONUL (UNITED KINGDOM,1999)

Seven Pillars of information Literacy (ISPGEMP)

S. N.	Pillars	Process
1	Identify	Personal need for information.
2	Scope	Current knowledge and identify gaps.
3	Plan	Construct strategies for locating information and data.
4	Gather	Locate and access the information and data they need.
5	Evaluate	The research process compares to evaluate data.
6	Manage	Organize information professionally and ethically.
7	Present	The knowledge gained: presenting the results.

5

Library Cataloguing and Classification

CATALOGUES RULES

S. N.	Cataloguers	Born	Catalogue Codes	Years
1	Napoleon B.	1804	French Code , France	1791
2	Anthony Pannizi	1797	British Museum	1841
3	Karl Dziatzko's	1842	Munich code, Germany	1850
4	Charles Coffin, Jewett	1816	Jewett's Rules	1853
5	Charles Ammi Cutter	1837	Rules for Printed Dictionary Catalogue	1876
6	L A and American Library Assoc.	1877/ 1876	Prussian instructions- A.D. Osborn 1938	1899
7	L A and American Library Assoc.	1877/ 1876	Anglo- American Cataloging Rules	1908
8	S.R. Rangnathan	1892	Classified Catalogue Code	1934
9	S.R. Rangnathan	1892	Vatican Rules	1938
10	S.R. Rangnathan	1892	Dictionary Catalogue Code	1945
11	American Library Association	1876	AL A Catalog Rules: Author and Titles	1949
12	Library of congress	1800	LC Descriptive Rules	1949
13	IFLA	1927	int. Conf. on Cataloging Principles	1961
14	American Library Association	1876	Anglo- American Cataloging Rules-1	1967
15	American Library Association	1876	Anglo- American Cataloging Rules-2	1978
16	American Library	1876	Vatican Code	1927

	Association			
17	American Library Association	1876	Anglo- American Cataloging Rules-2R	1988

CLASSIFICATIONS

S. N.	Founders	Born	Schemes	Years
1	Konrad Gesner	1516	Konrad Von Gesner's scheme of classification	1545
2	Francis Bacons	1561	Francis Bacons Chart of Human Learning	1605
3	Melvil Dewey	1851	Dewey Decimal Classification	1876
4	C. A. Cutter	1837	Expensive Classification	1891
5	J.C.M. Hanson Library of Congress	1864	Library of congress Classification	1904
6	Paul Outlet and Henry La Fontaine FID	1868/ 1854	Universal Decimal Classification	1905
7	W. C. B. Sayers	1881	Grammars of Classification	1912
8	J.D. Brown	1862	Subject Classification	1906
9	J.D. Brown	1862	Library Classification and Cataloging	1912
10	J.D. Brown	1862	Quinn Brown Schemes	1894
11	J.D. Brown	1862	Adjustable Classification	1897
12	J.D. Brown	1862	Manual of Library Classification	1898
13	S.R. Rangnathan	1892	Colon Classification	1933
14	H.E. Bliss	1870	Bibliographic Classification	1935
15	Lenin Library Moscow	1862	Library Bibliographic Classification	1959
16	F. Rider	1900	International Classification	1961
17	FID/UNESCO	1895/ 1946	Broad System of Ordering	1978

COMPARATIVE STUDY OF THREE MAJOR SCHEMES OF CLASSIFICATIONS

S. N.	Description	DDC	UDC	CC
1.	Main Outline	DDC comprised of 10 Main Classes with 9 sub-classes and 9 sub classes of each sub class. That is beginning with most general subjects to more specific ones.	The scheme follows DDC except addition of some new subdivisions and signs of combination for relation of subjects.	Main classes are comprised of Generalia (1 to 9) and 26 Main Classes (A to Z) of both Science and Humanities. The first 13 classes comprise the Science & Humanities.
2.	Notation	Notation originally was pure; later on some letters have been used. Three figure minimum notations have been used.	Mixed notation consists of figures letters and other symbols. The decimal point is repeated after every three figure.	Notation is extremely mixed consisting of Arabic numerals, roman alphabets symbols and signs including colon.
3.	Form Division	DDC uses series of nine common form divisions and these with minor alternatives are used with same meaning throughout the scheme.	Form divisions (01-09) retain the original Dewey significance but have been redefined and greatly expanded.	In CC, common subdivisions use of lower case letters with decimal subdivisions where necessary.
4.	Mnemonics	The principle	Number	The scheme is

		mnemonics features are: Form divisions, Geographical divisions, and Language divisions.	building devices as well as auxiliary schedules are mnemonics features.	faceted one and enjoys considerable mnemonic quality by the use of common facets.
5.	Geographical Divisions	Geographical subdivisions are provided by the use of the numbers 930-999. Every continent, country and division of a country is given a number. It also provides period division.	Place sign (1)-(9) is a special table indicating physical places. (3)-(9) are regular geographical numbers of Dewey used without the initial '9' and within brackets.	Common geographical divisions have been marked by decimal numbers 1-95 and in some cases sub divisions comprising of five figures are used.
6.	Structure	Based on the scheme devised by Bacon and Harris.	Based on the scheme DDC.	Based on the traditional main classes listed under four zones-Generalia, Recently Main classes, Traditional main classes and Newly merging methodologies.
7.	Index	Relative Index-tried to locate the relative position of the different aspects of	Alphabetical Index is not so exhaustive and developed on the basis of	Shortest index found in any classification scheme and is specific one which does not

		subject at one place in the index and is very exhaustive.	chain procedure.	list composite subject.

6
Research Methods in Library and Information Science

BIBLIOMETRICS CONCEPTS AND LAWS

S. N.	Models	Founders	Years
1	Statistical Analysis	F. J. Colle and Nellie	1917
2	Statistical Bibliography	E. W. Hulme	1923
3	Librametery	S. R. Ranganathan	1948
4	Bibliometrics	Alan Pritchard	1969
5	Sciontometrics	Nalimo V. and Mulchenko	1971
6	Informetrics	Nacke	1979
7	Netometrics	Bossy	1995
8	Webometrics	Almind and ingwerson	1997
9	Cybermetrics	Madrid	1997
10	Altmetrics	Jason Priem , USA	2010
11	Zip Law	ZIP (Word frequency)	1902
12	Lotka Law	Lotka (Author's production)	1926
13	Bradford Law	Broadford (Scattering)	1934

BIBLIOMETRICS SOFTWERE'S

S. N.	Software	Creators	Country
1	Bibliometrics Toolbox (1987)	Terrence A. Brooks	America
2	Data View (1993)	Marseille	France
3	Bib excel (2009)	Olle Persson	Sweden
4	Bib Techmon (2002)	Seibersdorf	Australia

DATA REPOSITORIES

S. N.	Repositories	Founders	Programmes	Years
1	ETD	University of Michigan, Virginia	Electronic Theses and Dissertations	1987
2	NASSDOC	ICSSR	Electronic Theses / Indian Social Science Periodical Literature	1970
3	DELNET	NISSAT/SIR, India	Database of Theses and Dissertations	1988
4	INFLIBNET	UGC	N-List	1991
5	Vidyanidhi	University of Mysore	Digital Library of Electronic Theses	2001
6	NISCAIR (NUCSSI)	CSIR	Journal Titles in the Libraries	2002
7	DOAJ	National Library, Lund University	Open Access Journals	2003
8	IISc	etd@IISc	Electronic Theses and Dissertations	2005
9	ShodhGangotri	Shodhganga	Synopsis of Research topic	2009
10	Shodhganga	INFLIBNET	E-thesis /Dissertations	2009
11	CSIR	Unit for R&D	E-thesis	2018

DIGITAL /MODERN LIBRARIES

S. N.	Library	Founder	Years
1	Digital Library	William Y. Arms (US)	1994
2	Hybrid Library	Chris Rusbridge (D-Lib Magazine) UK	1998
3	WWW.	Tim Berner Lee (European)	1991
4	Semantic Web	Tim Berner Lee (European)	2001
5	Virtual Library	Tim Berner Lee (European)	2001

DIGITAL LIBRARIES BY WILLIAM Y. ARMS (US)-1994

S. N.	Library	Places	Years
1	National Digital library of India (NDLI)	Kharagpur, India	2019
2	Traditional Knowledge Digital Library (TKDL)	CSIR, India	2001
3	Punjab Digital Library	Nanakshahi Trust, Chandigarh	2009
4	Open access in India	Delhi	2004
5	Digital South Asia Library	USA	2000
6	IGNCA Digital Library	DELHI	1999
7	TIFR Digital Library initiative	IEEE and Springer	2018
8	E-Prints at IISc	Bangalore	2004

HYBRID LIBRARIES BY CHRIS RUSBRIDGE (D-LIB MAGAZINE) UK =1998

S. N.	Library	Founder	Years
1	AGORA- Hybrid Libraries	London	1998
2	BUILDER- Hybrid Libraries	UK	1999
3	HEADLINE - Hybrid Libraries	UK	2001
4	HYLIFE - Hybrid Libraries	UK	2001
5	MALIBU - Hybrid Libraries	London	1999

VIRTUAL LIBRARIES BY TIM BERNERS LEE (EUROPEAN)-2001

S. N.	Library	Founder	Years
1	Intute (http://www.intute.ac.uk)	UK	2006
2	National institute of Science & Technology (NIST) Virtual library	UK	2009
3	Thailand WWW Virtual Library	Thailand	2008
4	The Virtual Library of Resources About Engineering	Thailand	1994

THE SPIRAL OF SCIENTIFIC METHOD BY DR. S. R. RANGNATHAN

S. N.	Methods	Phase Explains
1	Nadir---------------- ----Ascendant	Experimental Phase
2	Ascendant -------------Zenith	Hypothesizing
3	Zenith------------------ -Descendant	Deductive Phase
4	Descendant------------ Nadir	Verification Phase

TYPES OF BLOGS-1999

S.N.	Types	Means
1	Linklog	A blog comprising links.
2	Moblog	A blog written by a mobile phone or Personal Digital Assistant (PDA).
3	Photoblog	A blog comprising photos.
4	Podcasting	Blog containing audio.
5	Vlog	A blog comprising videos.

THE INDEST ACTIVITIES

S.N.	Electronic Resources	Explains
1	Access to Full text E-Resources	The access is provided to many online journals such as e-book, including Elsevier's Science Direct.
2	Access to Bibliographic Database	MathSciNet <http://www.ams.org/mathscinet>, SciFinder Scholar http://www.cas.org/SCIFINDER/SCHOLAR/index.html>, Web of Science <http://isiknowledge.com>, etc.
3	Access to Portal	Provides access to J-Gate Custom Content for Consortia.
4	Access to Open Access Resources	It includes access to Open Access E-Journals, Open Access Directories, etc.
5	Search and Browsing Facility	The browse and search interface allows to search e-journals and Backfills subscribed under the consortium for various categories of institutions.

6	Training Programm es	The training programmes are organized in a distributed mode wherein all IITs, IIMs and IISc Bangalore may conduct training programme for the member institutions with financial support from INDEST-AICTE Consortium.
7	Mailing Lists and Forum	The Consortium has an active mailing list and a Web site hosted at the IIT Delhi.

TYPES OF BIBLIOMETRIC STUDIES

S.N.	Types	Studies
1	Citation analysis	Authorship study, types of document used, language of the cited documents, ranking of journals and books, subject dispersion, obsolescence and citation half-life and self-citation etc.
2	Literature study	Growth of literature, growth models, methods of growth studies.
3	Authorship pattern	Types of authorship studies, techniques of authorship studies, author's collaboration.
4	Core journals study	Concepts of core journals, bradford's law, impact factor and immediacy index of journals, techniques of core journals analysis.
5	Core books study	Concepts of core books, techniques of core books study.
6	Subject dispersion study	Methods of subject dispersion study.
7	Internet data base study	Internet and Informetrics laws and methods study.

ONLINE COMPUTER LIBRARY CENTRE (OCLC), USA-1967

S.N.	Functions and Activities	Explains
1	Cataloguing and Metadata	OCLC offers full-service online cataloguing, simple copy cataloguing, MARC record collections, offline

		cataloguing, customized OCLC cataloguing from library's materials vendor, and automated copy cataloguing.
2	Dewey Decimal Classification System	OCLC administers the Dewey Decimal Classification system, the most widely used library classification system in the world.
3	Open WorldCat	WorldCat is the world's largest bibliographic database. The Open WorldCat programme makes it feasible to internet users who broadly search the Web.
4	OCLC Research	OCLC's 25-year-old Research arm furthers the science of librarianship by incubating new information access and exchange technologies, sponsoring the work of library scientists.
5	Digitization and Preservation	OCLC's digitization, microfilm and archival services are designed to protect, share, and manage collections.
6	Standardization	OCLC Terminologies Service provides single interface to access multiple thesauruses.
7	Publication	OCLC regularly develops and publishes studies and other informational documents that all libraries can use for "future-forward" planning.
8	Mailing Lists and Forum	"WebJunction" is a Web-based community dedicated to the emerging technology and training needs of librarians.
9	Others	NetLibrary provides full-text digital books, journals, newspapers and other published works in hundreds of subject areas.

INTERNET BROWSING AND SEARCHING

S.N.	(A)Browsing	Explains
1	Working with Address box of	In the online mode one can use web browser for arriving at a particular

	the Browser	address.
2	Working with Mouse	While we are on a webpage, we can use the vertical or horizontal scroll bars to move around or through a document.
3	Working with Keyboard Keys	We can use "Up" ( ) and "Down" ( ) arrow keys to move up or down one line. Pressing the "Page Up" (PgUp) key moves up one window length, and pressing "Page Down" (PgDn) moves down one window length.
4	Working with Hyperlink in the Document	A webpage contains many hyperlinks in the form of text as well as images.
5	Working with Back, Forward button of the Browser	If you browse through several pages in a window, you can move backward and forward by clicking the "Back" ( ) and "Forward" ( ) button in the standard toolbar.
	(B) Searching	Explains
6	Keyword Search	This is most generally used over the web. In this technique, the document available in the WWW is generally searched by using keywords in the search.
7	Phrase Search	When a user is quite aware of all the words that occur in the same sequence in the relevant digital document, then he/she can use phrase (or proximity) search techniques.
8	Wild Card / Truncation Search	When a user is aware only of some of the letters that are contained in the keywords then he / she can use wild card search technique to retrieve all the documents containing the words which again contain the particular letters stated by the user.
9	Boolean Search	Most of the search engines use "and" "or" and "not" as Boolean search query, some uses "*", "+" and "-" for the same purpose.
10	Natural Language	Some search engine uses natural language

	Search	search queries i.e. the user is free to use natural language query to retrieve the relevant result.
11	Complex Search	In this type, combinations of the above search techniques are used to retrieve more relevant results.
12	Field Search	A web page is composed of a number of fields, such as title, domain, host, URL, and link. So, field searching is one of the most effective techniques for narrowing results.
13	Meta Search	The content of search engines, indexes and databases generally vary. So, if the same search query is typed into several search engines then it is likely to produce different results.
14	Database Searching	Searching the directory or database is entirely a new experience. One can search the directory or databases by the specific entry point, which the particular directory or database is using to search its records.

TYPES OF RESEARCH

S.N.	Types	Means
1	Basic Vs Applied	Fundamental research is also known as pure research, theoretical research or basic research.
2	Descriptive Vs. Analytical Research	Descriptive research includes surveys and fact findings enquiries of different kind.
3	Quantitative Vs. Qualitative Research	Quantitative research is based on the measurement of quantity or amount.
4	Conceptual Vs. Empirical Research	Conceptual research is that related to some abstract ideas or theory.
5	Diagnostic Studies	The diagnostic study is concerned with the discovering and testing certain variables with respect to their association.

6	Explanatory Research	It structures and identifies new problems.
7	Historical Research	Historical research is that which utilizes historical sources like documents remains, etc.
8	Action Research	Action research is a reflective process of progressive problem solving led by individual work.

COMPONENTS OF RESEARCH DESIGN

S.N.	Steps	Explains
1	Title of the Study	The title or name o topic of research should be brief. In order to sharpen the focus if necessary a subtitle may be added to the main title.
2	Stating Problem	Stating the problem which surrounds the specific problem will provide a focus on the chosen topic for research.
3	Review of Literature	A review of the literature should be made.
4	Area and Scope of Study	The area and scope of the study should be stated.
5	Objectives of the Study	The objective of the study should be clearly mentioned.
6	Formulation of Hypothesis	Though it is not mandatory a few hypothesis should be taken.
7	Definition of Concept and Terminology	The concept and terminologies likely to be used in the research should be clearly defined.
8	Methodology	There are several methods of investigation and collection of materials.
9	Determining Tools of Data Collection	Determining tools of data collection and formulation of schedules or questionnaire.
10	Sampling Design	A complete coverage of the unit of the universe selected for research is not possible.
11	Data Analysis	The collected data should be processed and organized.

12	Limitation	Limitation in terms of gap in the data, sample should ascertain.
13	Interpretation of Results	The processed and organized data are interpreted for drawing inferences.

SERVICES OF JOINT ACADEMIC NETWORK (JANET), 1984-UK

S.N.	Services	Explains
1	Cataloguing	Up to 1988 many libraries become successful in providing their catalogue to the user through this network.
2	Database Service	JANET provides database services such as Cambridge Structural Database, Inorganic Crystal Structures Data File, Crystal Data Identification File, Agricultural Database, etc.
3	JANET OPAC	Through JANET OPAC one can access JANET catalogue and their database.
4	JANET News	This is a bulletin board service of JANET. Through which details of informative materials of all libraries linked in the network are provided.
5	Email Service	JANET began its operation with the inauguration of Email.
6	JANET and Internet	JANET was directly linked to the internet via the JANET IP Service (JIPS). This allows TCP/IP and JANET X 25 data on run over the JANET backbone.
7	Super JANET	It is a continuous up gradation policy of JANET for higher performance computing.

BOOLEAN SEARCHING

S.N.	Operator	Examples	Results
1	AND	Business AND ethics Cookery AND Spain	Retrieves records that contain ALL of the search terms.
2	OR	Hotels OR motels www OR world wide web	Retrieves records that contain ANY of the search terms.

3	NOT	Java NOT coffee Clinton NOT	Excludes records containing the second search term.

PREPARED OF INDIAN THESIS STANDARD

S.N.	Thesis Standard
1	Title Page
2	Certificate by the Supervisor
3	Declaration
4	Acknowledgements
5	Abstract
6	List of Abbreviations
7	List of Symbols
8	List of Figures
9	List of Tables
10	Contents
11	Introduction
12	Review of Literature
13	Research Methodology
14	Data Analysis and Interpretation
15	Findings and Conclusion
16	References
17	Appendices
18	Index
19	Curriculum Vitae
20	List of Publications

HALF-LIFE OF DOCUMENT FORMULA

S.N.	Abbre-viation	Means	Equation
1	L	Lower Limit of the Median Class (class containing middle value)	$L + \frac{\frac{N}{2} - cf}{f} \times i$
2	N	Total Number of Citations	
3	cf	Cumulative Frequency of the Class preceding the median or sum of the frequencies of all classes lower than median class.	

4	f	Simple Frequency of the median Class	
5	i	The Class Interval of the median Class	

LIBRARY RESEARCH TERMS

S. N.	Library terms	Years	Explains
1	A hypothesis tested for rejection is		Null Hypothesis
2	A research design is		A series of sampling
3	A research paper is a brief report of research work		Primary & Secondary Source
4	A Universal statement is		Inductive Reasoning
5	Analytical Research		With Facts and information already available analyze and make the critical evaluation method
6	ANOVA Method was first developed		R.A. fisher (Multiple Samples Testing)
7	Applied (Action Research)		Finding Solution for an immediate problem concerned with actual life.
8	Best is the enemy of good' is said by		Voltair
9	Bhore Committee establishment		Central Medical Library India
10	Book Number is a part of		Call Number
11	Bradford's Law related		Law of scattering
12	Calculation of impact factor		Web Of Science and SCOPUS
13	Catalogue Tray contain		1500 Cards
14	Chi –Square Test		X2 Pronounced as ki – square a non parametric test applicable in large number of population used to compare observed data

15	Common test in research demands		Reliability, Usability, Objectivity
16	Conceptual		Related to some abstract idea or theory to develop new concepts.
17	Contextual Indexing and faceted taxonomic access system (CFR)		Lngwersen and Wornell
18	Conversation of set number is		Coding
19	COUNTER (Counting Online Usage Of Networked Electronic R esources) Launched	2002	Online Journals and Databases
20	Current Contents is		Indexing Service
21	Descriptive Research		Survey and fact finding enquiries description of the state of affairs Ex Pot Facto Research no control over the variables report only
22	Documentation is similar to		Reference Service
23	Dublin Core metadata initiative which is based		XML
24	Empirical (Experimental Research)		Relies on experience or observation alone is a data-based research to test hypothesis
25	Essential qualities of a researcher are		Evidence, Systematization of knowledge
26	Eugene Garfield study of		Citation indexing
27	Exchange of documents libraries is called		Resources Sharing
28	Explicit to explicit knowledge is		Combination
29	Explicit to tacit knowledge is		Internalization
30	First Diploma In Lib. &		Madras

	Inf. Sci. is		
31	First Time B.Lib In Lib.& Isc.		Aligarh Muslim Uni., India
32	Fish Bone Diagram will helps		The Relationship between problems and causes
33	Formula-Δ1 = K (S + Δ1124. K(S) + knowledge in a mathematical equation		B.C. Brooks
34	Formulation of fundamental law is		Pure Research (Applied)
35	FORSA it is a forum for		Astronomy & Astro Physics
36	Functions of hypothesis		Test Theories, to describe social phenomena
37	Fundamental (Basic Research)		Generalization and formation of theory to discover new but broad principles
38	Gazetteers bring information relating to		To Find the place
39	Good Research Report		Title of The Study Statement of The Problem Review of Literature Area And Scope of Study Objectives of The Study Formulation of Hypothesis Definition of Concepts Methodology Sampling Design Constructing of Questionnaire Collecting of Data Analysis of Data Interpretation of Results Reporting and Finding Conclusion
40	Half-Life of information by Charless F Gosnell	1944	Rate of obsolescence
41	Harvard and Cornell developed		SMART Informational Retrieval System
42	Historical Research		Based on past

			events/ideas facts and attitudes social insight and historical orientation is necessary conclusion and decision oriented
43	Hlaf Line of information implies		"As Information Ages, it is useless"
44	Hypermedia refers to		As "Dynamic" or "Time Based" as "Multimedia
45	Hypothesis an		Assumption Or Supposition
46	Hypothesis is		Speculation
47	I Wyer theorized	1930	"Conser- Vative," "Moderate" Or "Liberal."
48	Ibid.		Refers to the same author and source
49	Identification of problem is		First step starting the research process
50	In 1974, Paul Zurkowski given by		Information Literacy
51	India : A Reference Annual" was	1953	
52	INFLIBNET Initiative For "ıntegrated E-Content Ports: Gateway To All Learners" is named		E-Acharya
53	Ink blot test is	1921	Hermann Rorschach, Switzerland
54	International Encyclopedia of social science was		New York
55	International Who's Who was published		Annually at London
56	Interview is a		Tool Research
57	J-Gate is	2001	Electronic Gateway To Global E-Journal Literature
58	Jubilee Project is related to		User Studies
59	Kardex Systems adopted in libraries for		Maintenance Of Periodicals

60	Lotkas Law related		Author's productivity Y = C/X^n Frequency of authors making X contribution
61	Management in the proper chronological order		Henary Gant(1861), Juran(1904), Peter Durker(1909), Ishikawa(1915)
62	Mathematical formula sample size is		Taro Yamane
63	Mean, Median and Mode are		Measures of control tendency
64	Measure of asymmetry		Skewness and kurtosis
65	Measure of dispersion		Range, mean deviation and standard deviation
66	Measures Of Relationship		Correlation And Regression
67	Multiple choice questionnaires comes under		Closed Ended
68	National Library of Indian a critical Study by		D.S. Kesavan
69	N-List has been developed for		College Libraries
70	Non-Probability Or Non-Random		Accidental, Quota, Purposive, Convenience
71	Observation		Method Data Collecting
72	Observation two types		Participant & Non-Participant
73	Op. Cit.		"The Work Cited"
74	Operating System		Unix 1969, 2. Liux 1991, 3. Ms-Dos 1982, 4. Windows 1985
75	Pareto Chart will helps to		The Intensity of each problem in the control
76	Pilot study consumer-research		Study done on a trial basis
77	Pioneer of social libraries		Benjamin Franklin
78	Project MUSE	1993	Online Database of more

			than 200 Journals
79	Qualitative		Concerned with qualitative Phenomena aims to discover the motives of human behaviour
80	Quantitative		Based on measurement of quantity determine the relationship between the variables
81	RDA stands for		Resource Description and access
82	Reader Guide to Periodical Literature		New York (USA) By W.H. Wilson
83	Regional Library Centre	1974	
84	Repository Software was		D-Space , E-Prints , Fedora
85	Research design categorized as		Explanatory, descriptive and exploratory
86	Research design component of		Review Literature
87	Research Report		Preliminary Pages – preface, foreword, table of contents, list of tables and illustrations Main Text - Introduction -Subject Matter, Statement Of Problem, Objectives, ROL, Significance, Scope, Conceptual Framework, Methodology Adopted, Limitation And Chapterization - Analysis And Interpretation Of Data- Statement Of Findings And Recommendation - Conclusion- Suggestions For Future Research End Matter –

			Bibliography, Appendix, Index
88	Research Design (Blue Print)		Measurement and Analysis of Data
89	Research Hypothesis implies formation of		Tentative Generalization
90	Research is conducted to		Generate new knowledge
91	Research is working in a scientific way to search for		Truth of any problem
92	SAARC Documentation Centre	1994	India
93	Sampling is		Smaller Representation
94	Scatter diagram is		Graph showing x & y values
95	Schedule		Collection of data through questionnaire
96	Shelf Rectification means		Restoration of shelf order
97	Simple Random Sampling are		1) Stratified 2) Systematic 3) Cluster & Area 4) Sequential
98	Software is used for analyzing the data in research		SPSS, Ms-Excel
99	Solomon four group design		Combination Pretest-Posttest control group
100	Spin Label consists of		Class Number
101	State of the art study is highest level of		Technique or scientific field, at a particular time
102	Statistical Tool is used "cultivation of crops using"		F Test
103	Study carrels are		Researchers
104	T- Test		Binomial Distribution
105	Tacit Knowledge is		Highly Personal
106	Tacit to explicit is the process of		Externalization
107	Tacit to tacit knowledge is		Socialization
108	Technological	1987	Allen

	Gatekeepers		
109	Term 'Cranfield Studies' are	1960	Experimental Research, UK
110	Term "BESPEAKING" for		Reservation of book
111	Term "Formulation of Hypothesis" is		Selection of Research tools
112	Term "Knowledge Management" was coined		K. Wiig
113	The Biggest Catalogue-World Cat	1998	OCLC-1967
114	The Central Value of distribution is	•	MODE
115	The Curves is more peaked than the normal curve		Leptokurtic
116	The Father of punched cards		Herman Hollerith
117	The Guinness Book of world records		Handbook
118	The highest point of spiral method is		Zenith
119	The Maximum and minimum value of a series is		Range
120	The method of research useful study on measuring the action life periodical		Citation Analysis
121	The preliminaries research Report is		Introduction
122	The Term intellectual capital introduced		Stewart
123	The Term Knowledge worker coined		Peter Drucker
124	The Delphi Method by O. Helmer		Forecasting Method
125	Things, Property, Material, Action		EJ Coates
126	Trend Reports are useful to meet		Exhaustive Approach

127	Two Categories of as 'Explicit' and 'Tacit' knowledge		Michael Polayani
128	Union Catalogue (Indcat)	1996	INFLIBNET
129	What is correlation		The Variation of two or more variables
130	Who is known as Dewey Of Japan		Fujio
131	Xerography is also called as		Electro photography
132	Z- Test		Normal probability distribution/ used to judging

TERMS FORMULAS

S.N.	Words	Equations
1	Degree of Freedom	(R-1) (C-1)
2	Mean	$\frac{\sum X}{N}$
3	Standard Deviation	$\sqrt{\frac{\sum X^2}{N}}$
4	Chi-Square	$\sum\left(\frac{(O-E)2}{F}\right)$

7
Information Communication and Technology

INFORMATION COMMUNICATION TECHNOLOGY INSTRUMENTS/TOOLS

S. N.	Instruments	Authors	Years
1	Telegraph	Caloude Chappe	1792
2	Telephone	Graham bell	1876
3	Automation	D.S. Harder	1936
4	Cybermatrix	Norbert wiener	1948
5	hypertext	Ted Nelson	1960
6	Cyberspace	William Gibson	1984
7	HyperCard	Apple	1987
8	Www	Tim Berners Lee	1991
9	Semantic Web	Tim Berners Lee	2001
10	Coalition of Broadband Users and innovators (CBUI)	Michael Powell	2002
11	Net Neutrality	Tim Wu	2003
12	Web of Science	Thomson Reuter	2009

OPERATING SYSTEMS

S. No.	System tools	Years
1	UNIX	1969
2	MS-DOS	1982
3	WINDOWS	1985
4	LINUX	1991
5	WINDOWS NT	1993

6	Emulator System Software (IBM System/360)	1963
7	SEWAK offline Software	
8	Ommi Scanner (14 Languages)	2000
9	BABYLON Software (Translations)	
10	Cite Sear	1997

LIBRARY NETWORKS

S. N.	Networks	Place	Years
1	Online Computer Library Centre	Dublin (Ohio)	1967
2	Research Libraries information Network (RLIN)	California, USA	1974
3	Research Libraries Group - RLIN	Columbia, USA	1975
4	National information Centre(NICNET)	New Delhi	1977
5	British Library Automated information Service (BLAISE)	UK	1977
6	Joint Academic Network (JANET)	UK	1984
7	Education and Research Network (ERNET)	Delhi	1986
8	Calcutta Library Network (CALIBNET)	Calcutta	1986
9	Defense Science information Network (DESINET)	Delhi	1986
10	VIDYANET (Dedicated Communication Computer Net)	Bombay	1986
11	Consortium of University Research Libraries (CURL)	UK	1987
12	INDONET (India Data Comm. & Computer Network)	Hyderabad	1987
13	Developing Library Network(DELNET)	New Delhi	1988
14	Australian Academic & Research Lib. Network (AARNET)	Australia	1989
15	Scientific and industrial Research Network (SIRNET)	Bombay	1989
16	Information and Library Network (INFLIBNET)	Ahmadabad	1991
17	I-NET ((formerly VIKRAM)	Delhi	1991
18	RABMN	Delhi	1991

19	Pune Library Network (PUNENET)	Pune	1992
20	Ahmadabad Library Network (ADINET)	Ahmadabad	1993
21	Bombay Library Network (BONET)	Bombay	1994
22	Madras Library Network (MALIBNET)	Madras	1995
23	Bangalore Academic Library Network (BALNET)	Bangalore	1995
24	Mysore Library Network (MYLIBNET)	Mysore	1995
24	China Academic Library and information System (CALIS)	China	1998
26	Health Science Lib. and information Network (HELINET)	Karnataka	2002
27	UGC- INFONET	Bangalore	2003

LIBRARIES SOFTWARE'S

S. N.	Software	Founders	Places	Years
1	Sanjay	DESIDOC	New Delhi	1995
2	Grathalaya	INSDOC	New Delhi	2003
3	Suchika	DESIDOC	New Delhi	1996
4	LIBSYS	InfoTech, LibSys Corporation	New Delhi	1984
5	OASYS/Alice	Soft link	New Delhi	
6	LibSoft	ET&T	New Delhi	
7	SALIM	Expertise, Thiruchirapalai, UptronIndia	New Delhi	
8	DELMS	DESIDOC	New Delhi	1988
9	CATMAN	INSDOC	New Delhi	
10	E- Grathalaya	NIC	New Delhi	
11	Libra	Ivy System Ltd.	New Delhi	
12	Trishna	NISTADS	New Delhi	
13	IMPACT	CSIR, New Delhi	New Delhi	1994
14	SOUL	INFLIBNET	Ahmadabad	2000
15	TLMS	INFLIBNET	Ahmadabad	
16	Krvger Library Manager	Blitz Audio Visuals	Pune	

17	SLIM	Algorithims	Pune	1988
18	Librarian	Soft Aid	Pune	
19	Libman	Datapro Consultancy Services	Pune	
20	Tech Lib+	NIC/OCLC NIC SR	Hyderabad	
21	LIBRIS	Frontier information Technology	Hyderabad	
22	Loan Soft	Computek Computer Systems	Hyderabad	
23	NEW GENLIB	Verus Solutions Pvt Ltd	Hyderabad	2007
24	NILIS	ASMITA Consultants	Bombay	
25	Library Manager	System Data Control Pvt.	Bombay	
26	MINISIS	IDRC, SNDT, women Unive rsity	Bombay	
27	Archives(l,2,3)	Microfax Electronic; Systems	Bombay	
28	Golden Libra	Golden Age Software Technologies	Bombay	
29	NILIS	Asmita Consultants	Bombay	
30	Slim 1.1	Algorythms	Bombay	
31	Tulib	Tata Unisys Ltd.	Bombay	
32	WILSYS	WIPRO	Bangalore	1998
33	Library Management	Raychansysmatics	Bangalore	
34	ListPlus	Computer Systems	Bangalore	
35	Liberator	CMC	Calcutta	
36	Acquas	Ober information System (Ascat, Ascir, Asire, Seras)	Calcutta	
37	Maitrayee	CMC Ltd. (CALIBNET Project)	Calcutta	1995
38	Tulips	Tata UNISIS	Noida, U.P.	1992
39	NIRMALS	Nirmal inst. Of Computer Expertise	Thiruchirap alai	

40	MECSYS	MECON	Ranchi	
41	OASIS for DOS	Soft Link	Australia	1983
42	FEDORA (199)	Cornell University of Virginia	USA	1997
43	CSD/ISIS	UNESCO	Paris, France	1985
44	Greenstone	Digital Lib. Project Uni of Waikato	New Zealand	1997
45	Koha	Kipto Communication Ltd	New Zealand	2000
46	E-prints	University Of Southampton, Uk	UK	2000
47	D-space	Mit And Hp Labs (Communities)	USA	2002
48	Evergreen	GNU, GPL (open source library management software)	New Zealand	2006
49	FireFly	Complete Public Library system, PERL	India	2003
50	WEBLIS	Institute for Computer and information Engineering (ICIE),	Poland	
51	Librarika	Rayhan	Bangladesh	2015
52	Alice for Windows		New Delhi	1985
53	Virtua (VTLS)	Virginia-Tech Library System		1997
54	Pro Quest	University Microfilms (E- Aggregator)	USA	1938

MEASUREMENT OF INFORMATION: INFORMATION COMMUNICATION TECHNOLOGY

S. N.	Measurements	Information Terms
1	1 Bit	Binary Digit
2	8 Bits	1 Byte
3	1024 Bytes	1 Kilobyte
4	1024 Kilobytes	1 Megabyte

5	1024 Megabytes	1 Gigabyte
6	1024 Gigabytes	1 Terabyte
7	1024 Terabytes	1 Petabyte
8	1024 Petabytes	1 Exabyte
9	1024 Exabytes	1 Zettabyte
10	1024 Zettabytes	1 Yottabyte
11	1024 Yottabytes	1 Brontobyte
12	1024 Brontobytes	1 Geopbyte

COMPUTER HIGH LEVEL LANGUAGES

S.N.	Languages	Founders	Years
1	Compiler	Grace Hopper	1952
2	FORTRON (Formula translation)	John Backus	1957
3	Cobol (Common Business Oriented Language)	Grace hopper	1959
4	Algol Language	Friedrich L. Bauer	1960
5	BASIC (Beginners All Purpose Symbolic Instruction Code)	Kemeny & Kurtz	1964
6	Pascal	Nicklaus	1971
7	C	Ritchie & Kernighan	1972
8	C++	Bjarni Stroustrup	1989
9	Java (Internet based applications)	James Gosling	1995
10	C# (C Sharp, Object-Oriented Programming Lang.)	Hejlsberg	
11	Visual Basic	Microsoft	1991

CLOUD COMPUTING (ERIC GRIFFITH, 2016) MODELS

S. N.	Models	Servicers
1	SaaS	Software-as-a-Service
2	PaaS	Platform-as-a-Service
3	IaaS	Infrastructure-as-a-Service

CONSORTIA FOR LIBRARY AND INFORMATION SCIENCE

S. N.	Consortia	Years
1	Forum for resource Sharing in Astronomy (FORSA)	1982
2	TIFR Libraries Consortium	1999
3	ISI Library Consortia Deals	1999
4	STI Network for resource sharing amongst S&T libraries	1999
5	DAE Consortium	2001
6	IIM Libraries Consortia	2001
7	JCCC & VIC	2002
8	CSIR E-Journal Consortium	2002
9	INDEST-AICTE Consortium	2003
10	RGUHS-Health Science Library and information Network (HELINET)	2003
11	UGC-INFONET Digital Library Consortium	2004
12	MCIT Library Consortium	2005
13	BJ Medical Consortium	2006
14	Consortium for e-Resources in Agriculture (CeRA)	2007
15	Electronic Resources in Medicine (ERMED)	2008
16	CSIR E-Journal Consortium now The National Knowledge Resource Consortium	2009
17	DRDO Consortium	2009
18	DeLCON Consortium	2009
19	National Library and information Services infrastructure for Scholarly Content (N-List)	2009
20	E-Shodhsindhu	2016
21	ICICI Knowledge Park (Hyderabad and Bangalore)	2016
22	e-Krishi Samvad	2017

USED FOR FILE FORMATS

S.N.	Formats	File Extension
1	Archos Reader	.aeh
2	Document file	.doc
3	Hypertext	.html
4	Open e-book	.oeb
5	Adobe portable document format	.pdf

6	Universal file	.rtf
7	Text	.txt
8	Word perfect	.wpd
9	Djvu- digital document format	.djvu
10	Epub (IDPF)	.epub
11	Fictionbook	.fb2
12	e-Reader	.pdb

INFORMATION COMMUNICATION TECHNOLOGY TERMS

S. N.	Library Terms	Years	Explains
1	1st Generation Computer		Dump Terminal
2	2nd Generation Computer		PC Work Satiation
3	3rd Generation Computer		Multi Media
4	4th Generation Computer		Dialog Web
5	A Research Paper is a brief report of research work based on		Both primary and secondary data
6	ADONIS (Article Delivery Over Network Information System) is		First Electronic Document Delivery System
7	Another Name Of Floppy Disc is		Diskette
8	ASCII Code consist of		256
9	Based on application types of computers		Super Computers, Mainframe Computers, Mini & Micro Computers
10	Bug is a		Error in a programme
11	Cache Memory is random access memory (RAM)		Computer Microprocessor
12	Calculating Machine is developed by		Pascal
13	CD-Rom is		A Process of information
14	CHECKMAT Software is		Serial Control
15	Chips is computer is made		SILICON
16	Content Management Software		Plone, Joomla, Jumbo, Opencms, Fedora, Drupal, Opensou

			rcecms, Alfresco, Dspace, Opencms, Kumera, Microsoft Office 365, Microsoft Live
17	Copy Tracker is software		Detect Plagiarism In Text Document
18	Dictionaries are		Lexicographers
19	DRDC is the first centre		Use Computer In The Library And Information Activities, India
20	Dynamic Ram (Dram) Dynamic Random Access Memory is a		Main Primary Storage Device
21	EDO Ram		Extended Data Out Ram: Much quicker than above two
22	EDWEB is		The Education Community
23	EEPROM		Electrically Erasable Programmable Rom
24	E-Journal Consortia was started	2003	UGC
25	Electronic Telecommunications System		Computers Together In Internet
26	E-Mail- Electronic Mail Early	1970	The Process of receiving messages electronically over the internet
27	Entireweb.Com is		A Search Engine
28	E-Prints is		A Repository Software
29	EPROM		The Erasable Programmable Read Only Memory
30	Expansion of worm		Write Once Ready Many
31	Expert System is		Computer Program
32	File Transfer Protocol is an		Internet File Transfer Service
33	First Electronic Computer is		ENIAC Stands For Electronic Numerical

			Integrator And Calculator
34	Folksonomy Means		Free Classification of information, Web 2.0
35	Gazetteer is basically a		Geographical Information
36	G-Index was suggested	2006	Leo Egghe
37	GUI stands for		Graphic User Interface
38	High Level - Programming Languages		Basic, Cobol, Fortran, Pascal, C,C++, Java
39	H-Index was suggested by	2005	Jorge E. Hirsch
40	Hypertext		A Hypertext Document is an electronic document that contains links to related pieces of information
41	Hypertext Transfer Protocol provides		A Web Browser to access a web server
42	Information Requirements of the social science (INFROSS) is		Experimental Research
43	Information Retrieval is		Fastest From Hard Disk
44	Information Technology good keeper		Allen Kent
45	International Standard Organization OSI model invented	1982	International Standard Organization, France
46	Internet was born	1969	APRANET
47	Internet was developed by		Us Department of Defense
48	Interviewing Research is widely used		Tourism
49	ISDN was first	1990	Singapore
50	ISID is		E-Bibliographic Database Publisher
51	Iso-9960 is related with standard for		Encoding Data On CD-Rom
52	Kuband		Satellite Communication
53	Library is a system		Various Sections as sub-systems coordinating.

54	LOCAS means		Local Catalogue Service
55	LOCKOSS (Software) is		Stanford University
56	Logical Operator "And", "Or", "Not"		George Boole
57	Lurn Q		Social Online Learning Platform For Learners And Teachers
58	Major Types of networks		LAN (Local Area Networks) WAN (Wide Area Network) Man (Metropolitan Area Network)
59	Mamma.Com is		Global Meta Search Engine
60	Microchip was invented by		Intel
61	Modular System of library building facilitates		Flexibility and Expansion
62	Mozilla is		Web Browser
63	Multimedia		Colour, Graphics and picture, and movies
64	Network Protocol are		HTTP, SMTP, TCP/IP
65	Neural Network is		A Programme
66	NICNET AND INDONET are networks		WAN
67	Opaque Paper is		Ultra-White Thin Paper
68	Open Software for library management are		Koha, Avant1, PHP and Mylibrary, Evergreen, Opal, Phpmybibli, Openbook, Openbiblio, Greenstone Digital Library Software (GSDL), Dspace, Fedora
69	Operating Systems is		IBM
70	PASCAL Language used in		Research
71	Patricia B. Knapp contributed on		Systematic use of user's education
72	PC/XT is		Personal Computer /

			Extended Technology
73	PDA stands for		Personal Digital Assistant
74	Peer Network Service is		Provide Service and to request service
75	Physical Entity of a computer is		Hardware
76	Pi is the e-book reading device by		INFIBEAM
77	Pre Coordinating Indexing System		Coordinated Prior to search
78	Programming Language are		Fortran, Basic, Cobol, Pascal, C, C++, Java
79	PROM		A Programmable Read Only Memory
80	Pure Notation used in		DDC-1876
81	Rangnathan' Canons Of Planes are		Ideas, Verbal and Notational
82	Research Libraries And Information Retrieval System	1978	California
83	RFID Technology is used		Thieft/ Circulation Control
84	Router is a		Device that forwards data packets between telecommunications networks
85	Sapling. info is		The Architecture, Planning & Landscape Information Gateway
86	Shannon and Weaver defined		"Information as essentially a measure of the absence of uncertainty"
87	SDRAM (Static Dynamic Random Access Memory)		Used Latest Memory Chip
88	Social Bookmarking Site are		Diggt, Delicious, Facebook, Orkut, Lislinks
89	Social Networks		Youtube (Video), Flicker-Photographs, Odeo

			(Podcasts), Myspace and Face Book
90	Static Ram (SRAM)		Small Storage Device With High-Speed Versions with mini buffer storage
91	Software is		Set of written programme
92	TCP/IP Transmission Control Protocol / Internet Protocol		Protocols Providing communication in a hydrogenous environment
93	Telex is		Communication of Text
94	Term "Shodhganga" is repository of		E-Theses
95	Ted Nelson created and coined the Term Hypertext in 1963.	1960	Project Xanadu (System)
96	Term 'Many Voices One World' by		UNESCO
97	Term "Web 2.0" was	2004	Dale Dougherty
98	Terms or Records In Marc Called		Database
99	The "Father of The Information Age"		George Boole
100	The 'Formulation of Hypothesis' is		Selection of research tools
101	The "Controlled Group" is a		Experimental Research
102	The 12 Rules for relational database is		Edgar F. Codd
103	The CD alphabets in CDS/ISIS stands for		Computerized Documentation
104	The Concept Of Artificial Intelligence (Ai) belongs to		Fifth Generation Computers
105	The Disk Into Tracks and sector is called		Formatting
106	The Essential Qualities of a researcher are		Spirit Of Free Enquiry, Observation And Evidence, Systematization

107	Types of Monitors		Cathode Ray Tube (CRT), Colour Graphics Adaptor (CGA), Enhanced Graphics Adaptor (EGA), Video Graphics Array (VGA), Thin Film Transistor (TFT-LCD), Light-Emitting Diode (LED)
108	The Journal Published in UK		Program
109	There are three ways for Transmitting Data from		(1) Simplex, 2) Half-Duplex, 3) Full Duplex)
110	Three (3) Switching System are		Message Switch, Pocket Switch, Circuit Switch
111	Three Switching Systems are		Circuit Switching – (Telephone) Message Switching - (Email)
112	Three Types of basic languages used in Computer Programming		Machine, Assembly And High Level Languages
113	Turntin Anti Plagiarism 'Urkund'		UGC, Bharathidasan University
114	Twitter is		Micro Blogging
115	Type of Transmission in cell phones		Microwave
116	Types of Computers		Analog And Digital
117	UNIMARC Follows The ISO -2709	1981	IFLA
118	University Providing open access to Sanskrit dissertations through internet		Delhi University
119	Unix is		Multi User Operating System
120	VERONICA is called		Grandmother Of Search Engines

121	Vivisimo.Com is		Specialized Info. Organ. Online Tool
122	Web 3.0 most important features are		Semantic web and personalization
123	What is DPI		Disc Per Inch
124	What is ESS		Electronic Spread Sheet
125	What is IRC		Internet Relay Chat
126	What is NAN		Neighborhood Area Network
127	What is Sco-Zenix		Multiuser Operating Systems
128	What is "LIPI" '		Word Processor
129	Who Designed Analytical Engine		Charles's Babbage
130	Wheat Loan Educational Exchange Programme	1961	
131	X.25 Type of protocol is used		Public Data Network
132	UBUNTU	2004	Operating Systems

8
Keyword and Abbreviations

Keywords	Meanings
Abstract	An abstract is a brief summary of a research article, thesis, review, conference proceeding of a particular subject.
Accent	Features of a person's pronunciation which help us identify where he is from, i.e., from a certain region or social strata.
Access links	Communication links that connect the user to the nearest switch.
Access Point	A name, term, code or other indexed characteristic of an authority or bibliographic record that helps make the record searchable. For example, titles, names, and subjects are access points.
Accessible	Content is accessible when it may be used by someone with a disability.
ACL	Agent Communication Language.
ACS	American Chemical Society. Producer of Chemical Abstracts.
Action Research	A type of practical and collaborative research to improve a method of Practice.
Adhoc Committee	A committee that formed for the specific/ special purpose.
Administrative Management	This approach seeks to systematically study the management process.
Aerosols	An air pollutant which refers to the dispersion of solid particles of microscopic size in gaseous

	media, such as dust, smoke or mist.
Aesthetics	The theory of the fine arts and the philosophy of the mind and emotions in relation to it; that branch of philosophy.
Agent	A computer program that performs a function that is normally carried out by an agency in daily life.
Artificial Intelligence	Artificial Intelligence – deals with techniques of making intelligent systems
Algorithm	Instructions for carrying out a series of logical procedural steps in a specific order.
Analet	Two or more isolates linked by relational operators according to J E L Farradane's Relational Indexing system constitute Analet.
Analogue	A term used to describe a signal, such as the human voice and electric current, whose value varies continuously with time or transmission method, such as the traditional telephone network.
Analysis	It refers to the conceptual analysis, which involves deciding what a document is about—that is, identification of different component ideas (concepts) associated with the thought content of the document.
Analysis of Information	It is a process of determining and isolating most salient information conveyed by an information source and separating this information in its constituent elements on the basis of predetermined evaluation and other criteria.
Animation	A technique in which each frame of a film or movie is produced individually, whether generated as a computer graphic, or by photographing a drawn image, or by repeatedly making small changes to a model unit.
Anomalous State of	Lack of a particular fact in the information see-Knowledge (ASK) ker's knowledge base, it may represent a much larger area of missing information, or it may represent a lack of knowledge structure.

Antiquarian Book	An old and 'rare' book, preferably 100 years old or more, similar to an antique. With common usage the term has come to mean any book that is out of- print, old, rare, scarce - virtually any book that is not a new or in-print book.
Antique Leather	Leather, dyed unevenly to look antique.
AOL	America Online is one of the largest providers of online services in USA. AOL offers to email, interactive newspapers and magazines, conferencing, software files, computing support and online classes.
AOSE	Agent Oriented Software Engineering.
Aperture Card	A micro-transparent document mounted on opaque card of 7" x 3" size.
Applet	A program inserted into a web page.
Application program	Program that has been developed to solve a particular problem, perform useful work on general-purpose tasks, or provide entertainment.
Applied Research	Distinguished from basic or pure research, any research undertaken to solve immediate or practical problems.
Aptitude	A combination of native and acquired abilities and other characteristics which can be regarded as predictive of a person's ability to become proficient in a line of activity with a given amount of training.
Arbitrariness	One of the properties which defines human language as distinct from animal communication, whereby 'Linguistic Forms' lack any physical correspondence with the entities in the world to which they refer.
Archie	Archie is a software for locating files on anonymous FTP sites. Archie is an indexing spider that visits each anonymous FTP site.
Archival Microfilm	A film having the information bearing characteristics retainable for indefinite period.
Archives	Public records or historical documents kept in a

	recognized repository.
Archivist	A custodian of documents or records relating to the activities, constitutions, claims, rights, treaties, of a historical figure, family, community, corporation, or a nation.
ARCOL	Agent Response and Communication Language.
Aries	Aries is an example of software that simplifies document delivery via fax.
Arithmetic and Logic Unit (ALU)	A part of the computer that performs arithmetic operations, Logic operations, and related operations.
ARPANET	Short for Advanced Research Projects Agency Network, the precursor to the Internet. Developed in the late 1960s and early 1970s by the US Department of Defence, as an experiment in wide area networking that would survive a nuclear war.
Art Paper	Smooth glossy paper, also known as coated paper. The base paper is coated on both sides with China clay.
Ascendant	A position of dominance, controlling influence, or superiority.
ASCI	American Standard Code for Information Interchange or ASCI is a standard coding technique for representing computer information.
Ask Jeeves	A unique search engine that combines a knowledge base of answers to roughly seven million commonly asked questions. This service is also in use at AltaVista.
ASP	Stands for Active Server Pages, a Microsoft's technology to enable HTML pages to be dynamic and interactive by embedding scripts, i.e., either VBScript or Jscript, Microsoft's alternative of JavaScript.
Assembly language	It is a low level programming language that allows a computer user to write a program using abbreviations or more easily remembered

	words instead of numbers.
Assigned indexing	The system of indexing in which terms are assigned by the indexer on the basis of the conceptual relations existing between them.
Assistive Technologies	Devices used by people with disabilities to access computers. Some assistive technologies include text-to-speech screen readers, alternative keyboards and mice, head pointing devices, voice recognition software, and screen-magnification software.
Associative Classification	It refers to the association of a subject with other subjects without reference to its COSSCO relationships and results in a relative index.
Associative Memory	A memory whose storage locations are *identified by their contents,* or by a part of their contents, rather than by their names or positions.
Asynchronous transfer mode	Mode of information transfer in broadband ISDN.
Athens	Example of Software that helps managing remote access provision to a large number of library patrons; Many databases and different vendors may be involved.
Attenuation	Loss of signal power caused by the communication media.
Attitudinal	Opinion, feeling or emotion concerning an event, fact or state.
Attribute	A setting for a tag, that affects the way the tag is displayed.
Attribute Value	The value assigned to a given attribute. Example: <name type="person"> here type is the attribute of the element name and person is the attribute value.
Audience	Grouping of audience into highly educative, non-technical, Analysis mixed type, international, or single group, or public at large.
Authentic	Genuine – Known to be true.
Author	The person, persons, or corporate body responsible for the artistic or intellectual content

	of a work. Usually distinguished from an editor, although these may be regarded as authors for purposes of cataloguing.
Authority File	Term synonymous with 'Authority List'. A list of all personal and corporate names of anonymous classic and sacred books, the titles of anonymous books and the headings for series cards.
Authority Record	A collection of information about one name, uniform title, or topical term heading. An authority record can contain the established form of heading, see from references, see also from references, and notes.
Authority services	The local government responsible for the provision of public library services in UK.
Autocratic Leader	Functions that managers perform and effective principles of management have been developed.
Automation	The organization of machine handling of routines or operations, requiring minimal human intervention.
Backbone	A high-speed line or series of connections that forms a major pathway within a network.
Bandwidth	The amount of data passing through a connection over a given time.
Bar Code	A bar-code sc.mer reads it as digital signals for entry in a computer database. Used in many firms of automated library circulation systems.
Base station	A wireless station covering a certain geographical area called *cell*.
Basic Research	Distinguished from applied research, any research undertaken purely for sake of knowledge without any immediate gain or use.
Behavioural School of Management	Also known as the behavioural sciences approach, the approach applies psychological and sociological theories, methods and techniques to the study of interpersonal and inters a personal aspect of managing.

Best Match	Searching databases on the criteria given by searcher that matches.
Benchmarking	The process of calibrating efficiency against other systems, getting the inspiration and building on others experiences.
Bibliographic	A collection of bibliographic data fields treated as one logical entity Record that describes a specific bibliographic item like as author's name, title, abstract, etc.
Bibliographic Instruction	Course-related classroom-based library instruction.
Bibliographic record	A record containing a structured description of library materials (i.e., book, serial, etc.). Elements generally included are: author(s), title, pagination, publisher, place of publication, and date of publication.
Bibliography	i) Serves as a guide to original research ii) Links all references on a subject at one place iii) Helps in retrospective literature search iv) Builds bibliography of bibliographies.
Bibliometrics	It is the application of various statistical analysis -to study patterns of authorship, publication and literature use.
Binary Search	A search technique for sorted data.
Binder's Board	A general term for pulped materials pressed into stiff, flat, smooth sheets of various thicknesses, used for the cover of a book, under the cloth, leather or any other material.
Bipolar	Representation of digital signals using voltages of different polarities.
Bit	When information is digitised, it is turned into ones and zeros.
Bit and Byte	Bit is short term for binary digit, the smallest unit of information on a machine. A single bit can hold only one of two values: 0 or 1.
Bit Depth	The number of bits used to represent each pixel. The greater the bit depth, the more colours or grey-scales can be represented.

BITNET	Short for Because It's Time NETwork. It is a network of educational sites separate from the Internet, although e-mails are freely exchanged between BITNET and the Internet.
Bitonal	Each pixel in a bitonal image is represented by a single bit, i.e. black and white.
Bits, nats and hart Bits, nats and hartleys	Units assigned to dimensionless measure of information depending on the base of logarithm used. *Bits* when the base is 2, nats when the base is e and hartleys when the base is 10.
Bleach	Removing or reducing discoloration in paper or cotton fabric by the use of acid or alkaline solution.
Blog or Weblog	A recent phenomenon of websites of individuals – where daily updates in the form of a logbook is common.
Blotter Paper	A completely un-sized sheet of paper made of rag or cotton linters, generally used to absorb moisture.
Book Cloth	A generic term for the woven fabrics used in covering books. Book cloth can be made of cotton, rayon or silk and is often backed with a layer of paper.
Book Jacket	A detachable protective wrapper for a book also called book wrapper, dust jacket, or dust wrapper.
Book Reservoir	A place either within the library or at a predetermined place within a region or country where weeded out documents can be stored or preserved.
Book Support	A piece of wood or steel placed at the end of a row of books to keep them upright. Also called 'Book end'.
Bookmark	A website address stored on a user's computer as a menu item so that he or she can easily return to it without having to retype the address, referred to as a 'favorite' in Internet Explorer.
Boolean	A system of three symbolic logical operators to

Operators	combine search terms to constitute a search statement, representing 'logical sum' (+) (OR), 'logical product' (x) (AND) and 'logical difference' (-) (NOT).
Bottleneck	Hindrance, obstruction.
Braille	Braille uses six raised dots in different patterns to represent letters and numbers to be read by people. Huis Braille (1809-1852) was a French teilcher of the blind.
Broadband ISDN	An ISDN designed for very high-speed applications.
Browser	User's software program for viewing & browsing information on the Internet.
B-tree	An indexed data storage method that is efficient for a wide range of data access tasks.
Buckram	A coarse, stiff cloth made by gluing two fabric pieces together. A thin transparent material is glued to stiff fabric.
Budget	An itemized list of expected income and expenditure for a specific future period.
Buffer Solution	Substances used for controlling the active and potentially harmful effects of chemical changes in materials.
Bulletin	i) A publication, generally a pamphlet, issued by a government, society or other organisation at regular but with significantly greater storage capacity.
Buttons	A button is a kind of icon which is stimulated on-screen and is activated by a mouse or other pointing devices to execute a command.
Byte	A group of data bits that are processed together. Typically, a byte consists of 8 bits. There are kilobytes, Megabytes, Gigabytes, Terabytes, etc. 1 Byte = 8 bits.
Cache Memory	A special buffer storage, smaller and faster than main storage, that is used to hold a copy of instructions.
CAD	Stands for Computer Aided (or Assisted) Design or Drafting, where in combinations of

	computer hardware and software is used for designing Products or architecture.
Calligrapher	A person who excels in writing beautifully and decoratively.
Campus Wide	Campus-Wide Information System is an information system Information Systems intended to present an integrated view of the institution to (CWIS) the members of its community, as well as to alumnae, prospective students and others.
Capture	A term used in document imaging for scanning of a document or any Other artifact.
Cardinal Scale	On interval measurement scales, one unit on the scale represents the same magnitude on the trait or characteristic.
Carrier	A high frequency signal that carries information signals.
CAS	Current Awareness Service.
Case	A book cover that is made completely before it is affixed to a book. Pasting a book into its cover is expressed as *'casing-in'*.
Case Sensitivity	The ability of a search tool to distinguish between uppercase and Lowercase letters.
Case Study	Intensive investigation of a particular unit.
Case Work	Developmental and adjunct mental procedure that follows diagnosis.
Cataloging Record	A bibliographic record, created from following the guidelines in the Anglo- American Cataloging Rules.
Catalogue (OPAC)	OPAC provides access to the library's holdings via a computer.
Online Public Access	Monitor, replacing the traditional card catalogue.
Catalogue Code	A set of rules for guidance of cataloguers in preparing entries.
Cataloguing in Source	Cataloguing books before they are published, the entries being compiled from proof copies made available by the publishers and the work

	being carried out by a centralized agency so that full cataloguing information is printed in the books concerned." (Harrod).
CATI	It stands for Computer Assisted Telephone Interviewing. In this system Computer is used to conduct interview.
CBIS	Computer Based Information Systems.
CCMB	Centre for Cellular and Molecular Biology.
CD ROM	Compact Disk Read Only Memory. A non-erasable disk used for storing Computer data.
C-DAC	Centre for Development of Advanced Computing, India..
CDMA	Code Division Multiple Access (CDMA) is one of several digital wireless transmission methods in which signals are encoded using a pseudo-Random sequence that decoded at the receiver's end.
CD-ROM	An abbreviated form of Compact Disc – Read Only Memory.
Cell	In the context of mobile communication, a cell denotes a small geographical area. In the context of broadband ISDN, cell is a small digital packet that carries information.
Cell switching	A switching technique in which information is cast in the form of small cells and transported over broadband ISDN networks.
Cellular Communication	A wireless communication technique in which a large geographical region is divided into a number of cells that are networked.
Cellulose	Organic substance that forms the main part of all plants and trees and is used in making plastics, papers etc.
Cellulose Acetate	The 'Safety' film stock introduced around 1930. Does not burst into flame in normal environmental condition, but does shrink and separate from the emulsion (image)..
Cellulose Nitrate	Film stock used prior to the introduction, of "safety" stock.. It decomposes, and can spontaneously burst into flame.

Censorship	Prohibition of production, distribution and circulation or sale of material considered to be objectionable on grounds of politics, religion, obscenity or blasphemy.
CGI	Common Gateway Interface is a way to allow users to provide information.
Chain Indexing	To scripts attached to web pages, usually through forms. A method of deriving alphabetical subject entries from the chain of successive subdivisions leading from the general to most specific level needed to be indexed.
Chain Lines	The lines that run parallel to grin of a sheet of laid or handmade paper, Usually two one inch apart. The lines are caused by the "chain wires" of a paper mould.
Channel	Established carriers that disseminate information of knowledge or any type of their surrogates.
Channel Capacity	The amount of information that can be carried by a channel with perfect Accuracy in unit time.
Channel coding	Coding for reliable or error-free communication via a noisy channel.
Characteristic Features	Set of elements or components that give a structural outline of a technical Communication.
Characteristics	Quality or an attribute with reference to which two things can be Distinguished.
CIMAP	Central Institute for Medicinal and Aromatic Plants.
Cinching	The wrinkling or folding over, of tape on itself in a loose tape pack. It Normally occurs when a loose.
Circuit	A two-way link comprising two channels, one in each direction.
Circuit Public switched	A switched network opens to public.
Circuit switching	A switching technique in which a dedicated path is established between end points for the entire duration of information transfer.
Circulation	A library service in which books and other

Service	library material are lent out for home reading 1 use.
Citation	Citation is a reference to a published or unpublished source.
Citation Analysis	Citation analysis is the examination of the frequency, patterns, and graphs of citations in documents. It uses the pattern of citations, links from one document to another documents.
Citation Index	An ordered list of cited articles (references), each of which is accompanied by a list of citing articles (sources).
Citation Indexing	Techniques of bringing together the documents (cited documents) which manifest association of ideas to establish the relevancy of information in a document (citing document) through mechanical sorting of citations in a citation index.
Citing Half-Life	The number of journal publication years, going back from the current year, that account for 50% of total citations given by the citing journal in the current year.
Cito-analytical	The document rehearsing the results of citation analysis.
Class and Class Limits	It is a decided group of magnitudes having two ends called class limits or class boundaries.
Class Range	Also called class interval is the difference of two Data Presentation limits of a class. It is equal to upper limit minus lower limit. It is also called class width.
Classification	The process of deciding the appropriate category for a given document.
Classification Plus	The Library of Congress classification schedules on CD-ROM.
Classification Schedule	The core part a library classification system which lists subjects in a systematic way along with their notation and some notes if necessary given against each.
Clearing house	An organization that collects and maintains records of research, development, and other

	activities being planned currently in progress, or completed.
Clicking	Clicking refers to pointing an item on the screen and then pressing and releasing mouse button.
Clientele	Users of the library and its services.
Client-Server	The Client-Server Architecture is based on the principle where Architecture 'client' program installed on the user's computer communicates.
Closed System	A system that does not interact with its environment.
Close Ended	They are also known as structured questions. These questions are having number of answers.
Clumps	A group of words that tend to 'adhere'. Various criteria can be used to define the boundaries of a clump.
Clustering	A group formation mechanism that combines a number of related terms. Four kinds of group: strings, stars, cliques and clumps.
Coal	Target set
Coaxial cable	Pair of conductors placed in the form of concentric cylinders along the same axis.
Code	A set of symbols for representing something. E.g., most computers use ASCII codes to represent characters.
Coded Form of Information	In this form, information is recorded using some codes. For example in the classification of books we provide information in coded form.
Coding	The digital representation of the characters.
Coefficient of Variation	It is a relative measure of dispersion which is independent of the units of measurement.
Cognition	The mental process by which knowledge is acquired through the mind.
Cognitive	Process of learning, understanding and representing knowledge.
Cohesion	Piece of writing where parts and ideas are fitted well so that they form a unified whole.
Collaborative Agents	Agents that work together to achieve a common goal.

Collaborative Filter	A personalized recommender for users on information obtained from other ideally likeminded users.
Collection	A group of documents that a user wishes to get information from.
Combustion	Actor- process of burning chemically.
Common Channel Signaling	Signaling done using a separate channel that is common to many information channels.
Common Isolates/ Auxiliaries	Known by different names in different systems, these are usually non-subject but recurring aspects of knowledge as embodied in documents.
Communication	It is transmission of a message by the use of effective language to achieve a predetermined objective.
Communication media	Media like copper and optical cables used in telecommunication.
Commu. system	Any telecommunication like satellite communication system.
Communication Transfer Chain	The process of transfer of information from generators to users.
Company Profile	A biographical account of a particular company combined with a description and assessment of its achievement.
Comparative Research	A type of descriptive research to compare two or more similar entities to highlight similarities and differences.
Compatibility of	Adaptability of Information Systems in various Information System environments.
Compendium	A short summary of the main points of a larger work.
Compiler	A language translator that converts the entire program of a high-level language into machine language before the computer executes the program.
Complex Paper Tears	A tear that has more than one top and bottom. A complex tear is usually two or more separate tears made over time.

Communication	Convergence of communication and computer technology.
CompuServe	A commercial online information network in USA, sometimes called CIS (CompuServe Information Service). CompuServe offers a variety of news, entertainment, special-interest services and Internet access.
Computer Animation	An art of creating moving images via the use of computers. Increasingly it is created by means of 3D computer graphics, though 2D computer graphics are still widely used.
Computer Tech. Network	It helps to get a glimpse of what is available with other computers on the network.
Concept	A general notion or idea of something formed by mentally combining all its characteristics or particulars.
Concept Searching	A feature that enables a search engine to find synonyms in its database.
Conceptual Instruction	An integrated system of concepts in a logically closed system.
Concrete	One of the fundamental categories propounded by Kaiser, which refers to things, place and abstract terms not signifying an action.
Condensed Form of Information	Information in brief provided in the form of summary, abstract, etc.
Consistency in Indexing	It is a measure that relates to the work of two or more indexers.
Consolidation	The technique of analyzing, evaluating, repackaging, sifting Repackaging information and finally putting it in proper perspective.
Consolidation of Information	It is a process of merging of information from one or more sources and presenting in a new arrangement tailored to the requirement of a specific clientele.
Consortium	A consortium is an agreement among similar institutions to finance a project which would be bear long for any one of them to bear the cost individually.
Content	It refers to tags, indicators, sub-field codes,

	occurrence identifiers, etc. Designator which describe or identify some attribute of a data element or group of data element.
Content Analysis	It is a method of data collection for studying events that have taken place in the past on the basis of literature.
Content Developer	Someone who authors web pages or designs websites.
Content Development	There are plug-ins for Internet browsers, graphics programs, and other applications.
Contextual information	Where informational value of a message is assessed based on a given context. Also known as pragmatic information.
Contingency Table	A two-way table to present bivariate data. It is called Statistical Inference contingency table because we try to find whether one variable is contingent upon the other variable.
Continuous Frequency	A continuous frequency distribution in formed Distribution where the variable can take any value between two numbers like height and weight, income, temperatures, etc.
Control Group	Group/population/subjects not exposed to any treatment. It also forms independent variable.
Controlled Vocabulary	A controlled vocabulary refers to an authority list of terms showing their interrelationships and to represent specific subject of a document.
Controlling	It is checking, verifying, testing, regulation and exercising restrain in order to successfully carry out a Management process.
Conventional Document	A document where the thought content is recorded in a natural language by means of writing, typing printing or by some near-printing process.
Cooperative Agents	Agents that help each other by providing the requested service.
Co-opted Member	Included in the committee by the consensus of the exiting I members.
Copy Cataloguing	Copy cataloguing involves taking original catalogue records that have already been

	created by other libraries' databases.
Copy Editing	Placing instructions in code on the manuscript for the printer: indication of typeface, italics, capitalization, order and relative importance of headings, etc.
Copyright	Legal measure which secures for limited time to exclusive right to authors and inventors to their writings and discoveries. 13 The Editor.
Corporate Writing	Technical writing in corporate bodies such as government and its agencies, institutions, learned societies, professional associations and others.
Correspondence	Special type of writing connected with specific functions of professional management.
COSSCO Relationships	It refers to Coordinate-Superordinate-Subordinate-Collateral relationships in organizing classification.
Cost Benefit Analysis	It is relating the cost of providing a particular service to the benefits produced by this service.
Cost Effectiveness	It relates to measures of cost to measures of effectiveness.
Cost-benefit	It is the evaluation of the worth of the system by relating the cost of providing the service to the benefits of having the service available.
Courseware	There is a wide variety of courseware resources available Directories via the Internet. These are very valuable resources.
Covert Observation	In this type of observation the participants do not know that they are being observed
CPM	Critical Path Method - a network analysis technique.
Crash	A course, open weave, starched cotton material, sometimes napped on one side, and used in library
Creative	Having power to create intelligence and imagination not merely mechanical skill.
Creative Writing	Writing that is built mainly on intuition feelings and imagination. The writers in this area should have a flair for writing.

Creativity	Refers to the capacity of human beings to produce and understand an indefinitely large number of sentences, most of which they might not have heard or used before.
Crop	The process of elimination of a portion of a picture, illustration or photograph that contain unnecessary material or to highlight a certain area of the image.
CSNET	Computer+Science Network was a large computer network, mostly in the U.S. but with international connections.
CSS	Stands for Cascading Style Sheets; when attached to documents. They describe how the document is displayed or printed, e.g., a CSS sheet is attached to an HTML document.
Cultural Transmission	Property of human `Language' whereby, the ability to speak a language is transmitted from generation to generation by a process of learning, and not genetically.
Current Awareness	i) Selectively cites relevant literature of high quality ii) Alerts users on new developments and trends iii) Avoids repetition and duplication of research report.
Curriculum	All the courses of study in a school, college, university, etc.
Cybernetics	Study of mechanical-electrical communication systems such as computing systems.
Cyberspace	It is an imaginary place where data, messages, pictures, sound, etc. exist in digital form.
e-book	A book in electronic form. e-newspaper : A newspaper in electronic form.
Cyclical Variations	Oscillatory movements of a time series where the period Statistical Techniques of oscillation, called cycle, is more than a year.
DARPA	Short for Defence Advanced Research Projects Agency, the DARPA is an agency of the U.S. Department of Defence that sponsored development of the protocols that became the TCP/IP suite.

Data	Raw numbers or letters stored in a computer which represent facts about entities.
Data Archives	A data archive is a permanent, electronic collection of datasets with accompanying metadata such that users of the data can acquire, understand, and use the data.
Data Bank	A comprehensive file of data which is usually stored on a direct access storage device.
Data Compilation	The regular and systematic recording of information discovered in a variety of miscellaneous collection.
Data Encryption	It is a security procedure that encodes data so that it cannot easily be understood.
Data Independence	Separates the data from the program, which often enables data definition to be changed without altering the program.
Data Integrity	Keeping accurate data which means few errors and the data reflect the true state of a database.
Data Layer	The layer on an optical disc that holds data as marks or pits.
Data Mining	Discovering hidden valuable information from databases.
Data Processing	The act of collating, tabulating, classifying and drawing inferences from the gathered data.
Data Recovery	The process restores the database to a correct state after a failure. It protects the database from inconsistencies and data loss.
Database	Information stored on computer files and accessible via a remote terminal and telecommunications link.
Datagram	An independent packet containing complete address information.
DDS	Document Delivery Service.
Deacidification	Treatment of paper or other library materials to neutralize acidity in order to improve durability.
Deciphered	To understand a written message.
Decision	Deciding what actions are to be taken.
Decision Making	The process of generating and evaluating alternatives and making choices-among them.

Deckle-edge	Book released by the publishers with rough uncut edges.
Decoding	Performing mathematical operations on coded signals to detect and possibly correct errors if any.
Deduction	A style of reasoning which seeks to explain any phenomena by arguing from the general to particular.
Default Syntax	A logical meaning of the use of space between the words when entering more than one word in a Web search engine carries out a search.
Degrees of Freedom	It refers to the number of pieces of independent information that are required to compute some characteristic of a given set of observations.
Dehumidification	In this process large, commercial dehumidifiers are used for drying the records.
Dehydration (chemical)	Removal of free or combined water from a compound.
Delegation	The process of assigning responsibility alongwith the needed authority.
DELNET	Developing Library Network (DELNET) has been established with the prime objective of promoting resource sharing among the libraries.
Democratic Leader	A person who tries to do what the majority of subordinates desire.
Demodulation	Extraction of base signals from the high frequency carrier.
Demultiplexing	Extraction of different information signals from a multiplexed stream of signals.
Dependency	A dependency refers to relationship amongst attributes belonging to the relation or different relations.
Derived indexing	The system of indexing in which terms are derived from the terms used in the text.
Descendant	Something that is going down.
Descriptive Metadata	Metadata that describes a work for purposes of discovery and identification, such as creator, title, and subject.

Descriptive Research	A spatial survey of an entity or a family of entities to study the existing status and state-of-the art.
Descriptive Studies	Research studies that are carried out to describe an object, phenomena, process, or organization in the present.
Descriptor	A word / term taken from a controlled vocabulary – usually a thesaurus – and assigned to a text to represent, partially or fully, the 'aboutness' of the text.
Desktop	Windows desktop is the basic windows working area.
Desktop Publishing (DTP)	Publications using computer software packages to manage or create the data to be printed, as well as that used to make up the pages of the final document.
Device Independent	Users must be able to interact with a user agent using the supported input and output devices.
Dextrine Glue	Water soluble gum prepared with dextrine mixed with water and other materials.
DHTML	Dynamic HTML is simply the combined use of both CSS and JavaScript together in the same document.
Diagnostic Research	A type of clinical method to investigate the root causes of a problem.
Dialect	A variety of a language, spoken in one part of a country, which is different in some words, grammar or pronunciation from other forms of the same language.
Dialog box	A dialog box is a box that appears on the screen and displays an option among the alternatives, for example 'Y' for yes and 'N' for no or typing the name of a file.
Diction	The choice of words or phrases in speech or writing to express ideas.
Diethyl Zinc	Agent used for mass deacidification. The process is being tested in the Library of Congress (USA).
Diffusion	It is a transfer process in which there is

	movement of technical know-how within a group of users.
Differentiation	Situations, i.e., formal, colloquial, casual, informal style.
Digit processing	Processing of a telephone number at the telephone exchange.
Digital	Consist of numbers and numeric representations, typically binary numbers. Nearly all computers use digital technique for storing and manipulating data.
Digital communication	A form of communication in which information is represented and transmitted by one's and zero's.
Digital Library	Vidyanidhi Projects, Traditional Knowledge Digital Library (TKDL), Networked Digital Library of Theses and Dissertations (NDLTD), Centre for Development of Advanced Computing (C-DAC) Digital Library of Art Masterpieces.
Digitisation	The process of converting data and information into digital format is called digitization.
Digitised Form of Information	Presentation of information using the digits 0 and 1 gives rise to this form of information.
DirectHit	A system that monitors user's selection of results from a search engine. It counts results that are clicked most, and time spent by the visitors at that site.
Disaster Plan	A disaster plan is a document that describes the procedures devised to prevent.
Discipline	A branch of knowledge, subject of instruction.
Discrete Frequency	A discrete distribution or discrete series is formed Distribution where the variable can take only discrete value slike 1,2,3,..... Number of students in a university etc.
Discussion Lists	Also sometimes called a 'mailing list' or 'listserv'. A discussion list is circulated to a group of e-mail uses who are interested in a particular topic/ area.

Disguised Form of Information	Information is communicated using common language. The hidden meaning becomes apparent only to the person for whom the information is meant.
Displacement	A defining property of human language, whereby language can be used to communicate about events removed in time and space.
Dissertation	Dissertation is a small formal piece of writing on a particular subject, especially for the university degree.
Division by Discipline	Division of knowledge into broader areas of study such as Natural Science, Social Science, Humanities, and so on.
Division Library	A collection attached to, and administered by a division or a group of related departments of a university or college, usually with some form of cooperative arrangement.
DLI	Digital Library Initiative.
DNS	Short for Domain Name Server, used to map names to IP addresses and vice versa. Domain Name Servers maintain central lists of domain name / IP addresses.
Document	The system enables users to other copies of Delivery Service materials retrieved by online searches, either by direct dispatch of items by the host, or via an agent.
Document Delivery	Document delivery refers to the complete process of supplying a document to its ultimate user.
Document Profile	Records in a selected database used for SDI service.
Document Repair Tape	A commercial tape made up of a paper carrier and a stable acrylic adhesive.
Document Scanning	Document scanning is the process by which print and film documents are fed into a scanner and converted into electronic documents.
Documentation	The dictionary meaning is "furnishing relevant documents to substantiate a claim". The definition in LIS field is collecting organizing,

	recording, disseminating, etc. of micro-documents.
Document Type	Term that identifies the format, genre, used to classify a document.
Domain Name	The name of an Internet site, for example www.dell.com or www.indiatimes.com.
Dots Per Inch (DPI)	Dots per inch (dpi) indicates the resolution of images or printers. The more dots per inch, the higher the resolution.
Dragging	Dragging refers to holding down the left mouse button while sliding the mouse to a new position on the screen, and then releasing the button.
Drying	In this process the frozen records are dried in a vacuum chamber dried at temperatures below 0 C.
DSL	Short for Digital Subscriber Line. A method for moving data over regular phone lines. A DSL circuit is much faster than a regular phone connection.
DTD	Document Type Definition-this is the formal specification of a markup language, written using SGML.
Duality of	Property of human `Language', which sees language as being.
Dublin Core	A metadata element set intended to facilitate discovery of electronic resources. A set of 17 elements prescribed for description of web resources.
Dublin Core Metadata	Dublin Core Metadata Initiative - the body responsible Initiative (DCMI) for the ongoing maintenance of Dublin Core. DCMI is currently hosted by the OCLC Online Computer Library Center.
DVD	A high-density compact disk for storing large amounts of data, especially high-resolution audio-visual material.
Dynamic Content	Dynamic Content is automatically or dynamically generated web pages typically

	produced using information in databases.
Dynamic Range	The number of colours or shades of grey that can be represented by a pixel. Dynamic range is a measurement of the number of bits used to represent each pixel in a digital image.
E	Anything in electronic, or more exactly in digital form.
E-Article	An e-Article is any material shorter than book-length which is distributed electronically.
E-Book	An electronic version of a book which can be read through computer or any other device.
EBSCO	EBSCO is a provider of print and electronic journal subscription services, and is involved in research, database development and production.
Econometric	The application of statistical techniques to economic theories.
Economic Feasibility	Possibility in terms of money.
Economic Forces	Pressures on a business that result from the nature and direction of the economy in which the business operates.
E-Consortia	Sharing of electronic resources.
ECS	Electronic Clipping Service.
EDDS	Electronic Document Delivery Service.
E-Distribution	Electronic distribution refers to distribution of information, art, or software through the World Wide Web or FTP sites or, in some cases, through mailing lists.
Edition Binding	The binding of an edition or a number of copies of the same book in identical style, usually by mass production methods.
E-Editions	A particularly powerful application of digital technology to replace printed critical editions of primary texts.
Effectiveness	Various terms are often used such as efficiency, productivity, performance to denote organizational efficiency.
Efficient	Maximally utilizing the capacity of a channel by

communication	the use of coding techniques.
E-Journals	Electronic journals.
Elasticity of Demand	Measuring the impact of change in price on the quantum of demand.
e-Learning	The use of digital resources for teaching and learning.
Electronic	An online document which contains information about Newsletter the recent and ongoing activities of an organization.
Electronic Document	It refers to the use of electronic technologies in support Delivery Service of document delivery and inter-library lending activities.
Electronic Journals	A journal which is produced n an electronic format; sometimes the electronic equivalent of a paper-based journal.
Electronic Mail	The electronic transmission of letters, messages and mail memos through a communication network.
Electronic Publisher	A publisher that brings out publications in machine-readable form.
Element (Dublin Core)	A discrete unit of data or metadata. Example, Title, Creator, Publisher, Date, etc.
Element	An element is a fundamental component of the structure of a text document. Some examples of elements are heads, tables, paragraphs, and lists.
Elements (XML)	The technical term used in XML for a textual unit, viewed as a structural component. For example, title, chapter, section, poem, stanza, etc.
Elimination factor	The proportion of non-retrieved items (both relevant and non-relevant) over the total items in the collection.
E-Links	Hyperlinks can greatly enhance the value of e-publications, providing a convenient and very powerful means of cross-referencing.
Embossing	Decorate with raised design.
E-Monographs	Some presses are making printed monographs available for purchase or subscription in digital

	form.
Empathy	The ability to identify with the various feelings and thoughts of another person.
Empirical Knowledge	Knowledge based on objective observation and experience as contrasted from intuitive or authority centered knowledge.
Emulsion	A coating consisting of light-sensitive materials contained.
Encoding (coding)	Performing some defined mathematical operations on digital signals to improve reliability and efficiency.
End Paper	A folded sheet of paper of which one half is attached to a board of the book and the other forms a *fly-leaf.* (See *'fly-leaf).*
End systems	Equipments at the subscriber premises that connect to a telecommunication network.
Endowments	Giving a large amount of money or property for the use and benefit of an organization.
End-user	Refers to end-users having access to information and Empowerment having the necessary skills.
Energy form	Electrical, optical or electromagnetic energy
Engraver	A person who cuts or curves a text or design on a hard surface.
Enumerative Classification	A classification that systematically lists all kinds of subjects of past, present and fore seeable future.
Environmental Forces	External and largely uncontrollable factors that influence the internal structures and processes of organizations.
ENVIS	Environmental Information System set-up by Ministry of Environment and Forests, Government of India.
Epidemic Model of Diffusion	Diffusion process examined on the analogy drawn from the spread of diseases.
Epitome	A condensed account of any literary work. It contains only the most important point of a book, essay, article or other literary work.
E-Prints	Digital equivalents of off-prints, pre-prints, or

	post-prints.
E-Publication	The term 'e-publications' usually stands for digital versions of conventional forms of publishing in print.
E-Publisher	An electronic publisher is the individual, business, or organization responsible for distributing the electronic form of information, art, or software being published electronically.
E-Publishing	Electronic publishing refers to the distribution of information, art, or software in any eletronic form, usually on some type of physical medium.
E-R Diagram	Entity-Relationship Diagram. A diagram that shows associations (relationships) between entities.
Era	Period of history.
Ergonomics	The study of the relationship of human beings and In chines especially in terms of physiological.
E-Science	Broadly, any use of digital resources for scientific research. However the term is currently associated with a more specific agenda.
Estimation	It is the method of prediction about parameter values on the basis of sample statistics.
E-Theses	Electronic versions of doctoral theses. There are obvious arguments in favour of making these available (especially if publicly funded) in institutional or other Open Archives.
Ethnic	Related to a racial, national or tribal group.
Euphemism	The use of a pleasanter, less direct name for something thought to be unpleasant.
Euphemistic	Speech or word containing euphemism i.e., use of pleasant, mild or indirect words or phrases in place of more accurate or direct ones.
Evaluation	It is the comparison of actual results, with anticipated results on the basis of objectives of an information organization.
Evaluation of Information	It is a process of ascertaining and appraising the intrinsic merit, validity and reliability of

	information conveyed, comparison of information on the same topic from variety of sources.
Evolution	Process of organisation by development.
Exact Match	Searching databases on the topic of a phrase (a combination of words) entered by the searcher that exactly matches.
Excite	Regarded as one of the more popular search engines. It searches top search engines and compile them to give best possible results.
Exclusive Type Class	A class interval which includes all observations Interval that are greater than or equal to the lower limit but less than the upper limit.
Exhaustivity	Navigating in a database, choosing broader search terms to obtain greater number of references.
Expected Frequency	It is the expected cell frequency under the assumption that both the variables are independent.
Ex-Officio Member	Member by virtue of the office held.
Experimental Group	Group of population/subjects exposed to treatment and observation to measure the change. It is dependent variable.
Experimental Hypothesis	A prediction that the treatment will cause an effect.
Experimental Studies	Research studies that are undertaken to study cause and effect relations between variables are called experimental studies.
Expert Systems	A set of computer programs that guide the user to locate and use information.
Exploratory Research	A rudimentary or preliminary work to study the viability of the research problem for its successful completion and useful results.
Expository	A piece of writing that seeks to examine the theme through analysis or explanation.
Expressed As	Where Ii(JY) = Immediacy index of the journal J for the year Y; c = Number of citations received by x source items published in journals J in the

	year Y; x = Number of source items published in journal J in the year Y.
E-xtensible Markup	A subset of Standard Generalized Markup Language Language (XML) (SGML), a widely used international text processing standard.
Extension Work	The provision by a library of materials.
Extension Workers	Persons, who collect, assimilate, repackage and disseminate information. Normally, they function in rural and semi-urban areas.
External Environment	Social, political and economic factors that might affect an organization.
External House	The house journal meant for the external public like Journal the shareholders, customers, etc.
E-Zine	The "zine" is short for either "fanzine" or "magazine," Zines are generally produced by one person or a small group of people.
Faceted Classification	A scheme of classification which reflects in its structure the analysis of subject according to a number of fundamental concepts.
Facsimile	An exact copy of a document or illustration obtained by photomechanical processes.
Failure analysis	A diagnostic procedure, which involves the analysis of recall and precision failures encountered to the principal subsystems of an IR system.
Fallout ratio	It is the proportion of the irrelevant items in the file, which are retrieved by a request. The fall out thus represents the fractional recall of irrelevant items.
False Drops	Retrieval of unwanted items because of the false coordination of terms at the time of searching. The standard text-formatting language for documents.
FAO	Food and Agricultural Organization.
FAQ	Frequently Asked Questions.
Feathered Edge	The fuzzy effect resulting from water or needle tearing a piece of Japanese repair tissue.
Feedback	The act of using output from a system as part of input to the system to achieve a greater

	operational efficiency in the performance of the system.
Field	Collection of data elements that together make up a unit of information. A field contains data elements such as the name of the author, title of the document, imprint, etc.
Field-Specific search	A search facility that allows the searcher to specify the field (e.g. Title field) in which a search term should be present.
File Transfer	File transfer is a common method of moving files between two Internet sites. FTP is a special way to login to another Internet site for the purposes of retrieving and / or sending files.
File Transfer Protocol (FTP)	The protocol used on the Internet for exchanging files.
Filtering Service	Recent from of SDI, especially for news I&RS : Information & Referral Service.
Finishing	This Comprises lettering, tooling and polishing.
Fire Wall	A combination of hardware and software that separates a LAN into two or more parts for security purposes.
Fixed Costs	Costs which do not vary with sales/services value.
Fixed Field	A field which has predetermined length and it cannot accommodate more characters than the specified earlier.
Flip Charts	Flip charts are widely used in industry. They are portable, require no special equipment, and do not require darkening the room.
Flow Diagram	A flow diagram is a graphic view of a work area upon which is superimposed the path or movement of workers or the flow of materials.
Flow Process Chart	It is a graphic means of potraying the work involved in a job where the person or process charted moves from place to place.
Fluorescent	The property of some substances of emitting when exposed to radiation, rays of greater wavelength than those received.
Fly-leaf	A blank leaf at the beginning and at the end of

	a book.
Foggy	Idea of confused nature.
Folding Strength	The basic material that create paper is fibre. The length, intrinsic strength and the direction of the fibres relative to the line of folding are the factors.
Folio	A full sheet of paper folded once to give four pages. (See also *Quarto, Octavo,).*
Font	A font, strictly speaking, is a set of characters that all belong to the same size and style of a typeface. For example, Courier.
Fore-edge	The edge of a book opposite the spine (See also *spine).*
Foreign Key	A column in one table that is primary key in a second table. It does not need to be a key in the first table:
Formal Organisation	An organisation with a well defined structure, clearly specified jobs for members, and a hierarchy of objectives.
Format	Arrangement or presentation of data in the record.
Forms	The mechanism by which web pages become interactive, allowing users to supply input to CGI or other scripts.
Forth Estate	A group (here the Media) other than the usual constitutional powers, like the legislative, executive and judiciary of a state that wields influence in the politics of a country
Fourier analysis	Analysis of complex waveform in terms of simple pure waves.
Foxing	Brown-red stains found on paper. the origins of the marks are not yet fully understood, but they occur in books and documents stored in an uncared environment.
FRBR	(Functional Requirements for Bibliographic Records) A conceptual data model for bibliographic database design and management. The model, proposed by IFLA
Frequency Curve	It is a smoothened graph of a frequency

	distribution obtained from frequency polygon through free hand tracing in such a way that the area under both of them is approximately the same.
Frequency Polygon	It is a broken line graph to represent a frequency distribution and can be obtained either from a histogram or directly from the distribution.
Frequency spectrum	Range of frequencies in telecommunication systems.
Frontispiece	It is an illustration (photograph, map, etc.) that usually faces the title page of a book.
FSO	Full text Sources Online - A directory published twice a year by Information Today Inc, USA.
FTP	File Transfer Protocol, a common method of moving files between two Internet sites.
Fully connected network	A network in which all communicating entities are directly connected with each other.
Fumigate	Destroy infectious germs, insects etc. with the fumes of certain chemicals.
Fumigation	Exposure to vapours or fumes for disinfection or destruction of bugs, rats etc.
Function	A type of work activity that can be identified and distinguished from other work.
Fungi	Type of plant without leaves, flowers or green colouring matter growing on other plants or decaying matter.
Fungicides	Substance that kills fungus.
Fungus	A type of plant without leaves, flowers, or green colouring matter, growing on other plants or decaying matter.
Fungus Spores	Destructive mildews flourishing in damp conditions. They appear in dull shades of green, gray, brown, blue and purple.
Fuzzy Retrieval	The capability to locate spellings of words that are similar to the entered search term. Fuzzy retrieval increases recall and decreases precision.
Gang Chart	A type of flow process chart that has been

	modified to show processes involving the movement of more than one person or product.
Gantt Chart	A two dimensional graph with time on the horizontal axis and a listing of the parts of a program on the vertical axis.
GARE	It stands for Guidelines for Authority and Reference Entries. It is a standard developed by IFLA to manage encoding of authority data and reference entries.
Gateway Service	A service allowing authorised material such as e-mail to pass between dissimilar networks, by dovetailing one network's protocol with the others.
Gateways	Any system permitting users of one computer system to access another.
General Classification System	A classification whose area of purview extends to the entire domain of the universe of knowledge, and for classifying documents in all media.
Generality number	It expresses the number of items relevant to a particular request over the total number of items in the collection.
Genetics	The branch of biology dealing with heredity.
Geostationary satellite	A satellite whose instantaneous angular velocity and mean orbital period are the same as that of earth.
Gestalt	A technical term in psychology. It is something that you see or think of that has particular qualities.
GILS	Global Information Locator Service.
GIST	Graphics and Intelligence based Scripting Technology (GIST) is developed by C-DAC, India. It supports major Indic languages.
Global Information System	An international venture in terms of coverage of documents, variety of services and products to users for achieving economy in terms of money, time and efforts.
Glossary	An alphabetical list of abstruse or technical

	terms concerned with any specific subject, together with their definitions or elucidations.
Glyphs	Particular shapes of a given characters as they are displayed/rendered on screen
GO	Government Order. A document of great importance for all concerned with the GO in question.
Gopher	A method of making menus of material available over the Internet. Gopher is a Client and Server style program, which requires that the user have a Gopher Client program.
Governance	An exercise of authority and control, inspect and supervise. Member Secretary : the member of the committee, who also worKs as secretary.
Grain	In machine-made paper and board, the direction that the majority of paper on cloth fibers lies. In cloth, the grain is the direction of the warp threads.
Graphic	A picture or illustration, also called image.
Growth Pattern	Process of increase in size and number with some consistency.
GSARE	It is a standard to set Guidelines for Subject Authority and Reference Entries.
Halftone	A method of generating an image that requires varying densities or shades to accurately render the image.
Hand Lamination	The process provides a coating of Chiffon and fixing cellulose acetate foil to it by means of acetone.
Handwritten Form of Information	Information written on a medium like paper. Before the advent of paper.
Hashing	An access mechanism that transforms the search key into a storage address, thereby providing very fast access to stored data.
Hawthorne Bibliographic Instruction	Course-related classroom-based library instruction.
Hawthorne Effect	The influence of behavioural researches on the

	people they study.
Hawthorne Elasticity Hawthorne Study	The effect of making people feel very special by changing their perception.
Hazards	Anything which might cause harm or create danger.
Head Band	This is a handmade of strong cotton of colored silk cards.
Heuristic search	User's search that gets modified continuously in the course search, in the light of knowledge gained at each stage of search results.
Hexadecimal	A numbering system which uses a base of 16. The first ten digits are 0-9 and the next six are A-F. Hexadecimal numbers are used to colc ır web pages.
High level language	Also known as the procedural language it resembles human languages such as English.
Hinge	The flexible part of the binding material (leather, cloth, rexine or paper) on which the book opens.
Histogram	It is a set of adjacent rectangles presented vertically with areas proportional to the frequencies.
Historicity	The quality or state of being historic as distinct from the mythological or legendary.
Hoist	Lift with an apparatus of ropes and pulleys or a kind of elevator.
Home Page	Originally, the web page that a browser is set to use when it starts up.
Homonym	A word having same pronunciation and spelling as another word but different in meaning and origin.
Hospitality of Notation	An essential quality of any notational system enabling it to accommodate new subjects.
House Journal	A periodical produced by a commercial or industrial organisation, either for internal distribution amongst the staff and employees or externally to its customers.
House style	Conventions used by a publisher when '

	preparing material for printing which may be different for different publishing houses depends on their needs requirements and preferences.
HTML	Hypertext Markup Language is the standard text formatting language for documents on the World Wide Web.
HTTP	Hyper Text Transfer Protocol, the conventions used by web browsers and servers to transfer web pages.
HTTPD	Stands for Hyper-text Transfer Protocol Daemon, a computer program, which manages the transfer of hypertext and multimedia, documents over the Internet.
Human Intellect	Skills of all variety necessary for all round development.
Human Relations Movement	The trend toward treating satisfaction of psychological needs as the primary concern of management.
Human Resources	People needed to operate the business and to perform those tasks that require human talent, skills, and abilities.
Humidity	Pounds of water vapour carried by one pound of dry air.
Hypermedia	A combination of hypertext and multimedia that allows users to move in a non-linear fashion through text, images, sounds, and other information.
Hypertext	A collection of documents joined by links so that users can read it in a variety of different orders.
Hypothesis	A proposition or set of propositions set forth as an explanation for the occurrence of some specified group of phenomena.
IAEA	International Atomic Energy Agency.
IARI	Indian Agricultural Research Institute.
Icons	An icon is a small picture or graphical display used to represent a command, a program or a task.

ICSSR	Indian Council of Social Science Research.
Idea Density	Number of ideas or concepts introduced in a text.
Ideogram	A form of primitive writing expressing a way of expressing Ideas, not necessarily in words, is called ideography.
Idiolect	The linguistic system of an individual speaker, i.e., her/his personal dialect.
IDS	Stands for Intrusion Detection System, designed to protect a specific portal, volume or area, using technologies designed to sense movement, sound or a specific act such as opening a door.
IEC	International Electrotechnical Commission.
IEE	Institution of Electrical Engineers (IEE), United Kingdom.
ILL	Inter library loan (ILL) is the process by which a library requests material from, or supplies material to, another library.
Illuminated	Many religious manuscripts and some of the others were ornamented in the early days by patterns and pictures done in gold paint and.
Image	A graphical presentation.
Image File	A file containing an image.
Image Sharpening	Scanned images can be adjusted to increase edge contrast and artificially enhance the overall quality of image.
Imitation Art Paper	Unlike art paper, which is coated, imitation art paper is loaded, by adding clay and glue to the pulp.
Immediacy Index	A measure to show how quickly the 'average article' of a particular journal is cited.
Impact Factor	A frequency with which the average articles of the journal has been cited in a particular year.
Inclusive Type Class	A class interval in which all observations lying Interval between and including the class limits are included.
Incunabula	Books printed in the 15th century AD., at the earliest stage of printing. These are the

	specimens of the cradle period of printing and typographic art.
Independent Study	Cognitive capabilities of user to access library resources and service independently.
INDEST	Indian National Digital Library in Engineering, Science and Technology. A consortium promoted by MHRD.
Index	A sorted list of key values from the original table along with a pointer to the rest of the data in each row.
Indexers	Programs that read pages throughout the web and add a description of their contents to a database that can be searched by users looking for specific information.
Indexing	The process of evaluating information entities and creating indexing terms, normally subject or topical terms, that aid in finding.
Indexing language	A language used to describe and search subjects in an index.
Indian MEDLARS Centre	A Centre jointly set-up by NIC and ICMR to cater to the information needs of medical community of India.
Induction	A formal process of introducing and training new employees on their job, position, or office.
Inductive Reasoning	Logical reasoning based on long drawn facts and observations. Sun will rise from the east tomorrow is inductive reasoning.
Industrial Engel Curve	Relates to probability of a firm having adopted the new innovation to the firms' size.
Inference Engine	A component of expert systems that makes decisions based upon reasoning built into the systems through factual or ruled based methods.
Informant	A person part of the population under study, who gives information or opinion to the researchers.
Information	Search and extract the requested information from Extraction documents.
Information Age	A period characterized by domination of

	information.
Information Analysis	The methods and techniques of identifying the essential concepts, which may be useful for the user's requirements.
Information Analysis Centre	It is a formally structured organizational unit specifically established for the purpose of acquiring, selecting, storing, retrieving, evaluating, analyzing.
Information Broker	An individual of a firm, who, on demand, seeks to answer questions using all available sources and who is in business for profit.
Information Consolidation	The responsibilities exercised by individuals, Activities departments, or organisations for evaluating and compressing relevant documents.
Information Desk	A desk in a library or other building staffed by one or more persons whose function is to give information.
Information entropy	Average information content of a message in a set of messages.
Information Filter	An essential mediator between information sources and their users.
Information Generation and Communication Facsimile Transmission	Transmission of an image over Communication lines in the form of electric signals.
Information Industry	Market place created by the convergence of computers, telecommunication and micro electronics.
Information Institutions Invisible College	An elite of high performing scientists who has an informal network of scientific communication and the published literature.
Information measure	Assessing the informational value of a message by using one of a variety of techniques.
Information Need	Are mainly psychological and consist of the processes involving the identification, analysis, and satisfaction at conceptual level.
Information	Library materials which are earlier read in the

Resources	reading room of the library.
Information Retrieval	Search and produce a list of documents that may contain the requested information.
Information Technology	Acquisition, processing, storage and dissemination of information by a combination of base technologies.
Information Transfer	A chain of activities, the main link being information generator, editor, publisher of primary publications, indexing and abstracting journal producers, libraries, documentation.
Information Transfer Chain	The movement of information from generation to use with a series of intermediate links that connect each other to form a chain.
Infrastructure	All institutional bodies holding information resources and facilities.
Injection laser diode (ILD)	An optical source that produces sharp light beam when current is applied to it.
Inktomi	A database of websites used by many search engines like Hotbot, MSN etc. Yahoo also uses Inktomi.
Input Devices	A device by which data can be entered into a computer system.
Input String	It refers to a set of terms arranged according to the role operators in PRECIS.
Input-Output (I/O)	Pertaining to either input or output, or both. Refers to the movement of data between a computer and a directly attached peripheral.
INSA	Indian National Science Academy
Inscriber	A person who writes or curves words on a surface especially as a formal or permanent record.
inspective conversion	The partial or complete conversion of an existing catalogue into machine-readable form, as opposed to converting records created Urgent.
Instruction Set	A complete set of the operators of the instructions of a computer together with the description of the types of meanings that can be attributed to their operands.

Instructional Materials	Writings that are meant to provide guidance in learning and using a system.
Instructional writing	Writings that aid the process of learning, teaching, application operations, etc.
Integrated Library System	A library automation system in which data entered in one module by other modules to avoid data redundancy.
Intelligent Agent	An agent that possesses certain attributes that are associated with human intelligence.
Intelligent Information	A system that carries out intelligent retrieval, i.e., the use, Retrieval System by a computer system, of the stored knowledge of its world of documents, users, etc.
Inter library loan	Library service which provide document circulation to the outside libraries as clientele.
Interface Agents	Agents that perform the functions of a personal assistant to an office executive.
Inter firm Diffusion	Spread of new process from firm to firm within an industry.
Inter-Governmental	International organisation in which the members are national governments.
Inter-library Loan	A book or other item lent between libraries.
Internal Environment	The conditions inside an organisation.
Internal House	The house journal meant for internal public namely Journal the employees.
International Standard	A unique identification number assigned to a work Book Number (ISBN) by its publisher. Each ISBN has ten characters.
Internet	A global network connecting millions of computers. More than 100 countries are linked into exchanges of data, news and opinions.
Internet Explorer	It enables user to connect the Internet.
Interoperability	Interoperability refers to the ability of information systems to operate in conjunction.
Interpreter	A language translator that converts each procedural language statement into machine language and executes it immediately.
Interview	List of printed questions for seeking answers

Schedule	from the respondents. Interviewer records the responses on it.
Interviewer	It is the person who is asking questions. He or she may be a research assistant or a researcher himself/herself.
Intrafirm Diffusion	Spread of new process within a firm.
Intranet	A network belonging to an organisation, accessible only by the organisation's members, employees, or others.
Intuitive	Feeling that something is true or exits, although one may have no evidence or proof of it. 18 Linguistics.
Inverted File	A representation for a collection that is essentially an index.
Invisible Colleges	A group of persons informally forming a group for exchange of information and ideas.
Invisible Web	It refers to those pages what we can't see in the results pages after we run a search on the Web.
IP Address	The address of a computer directly accessible on the internet by anyone. For example: 192.168.1.106.
IRC	Short for Internet Relay Chat, IRC is a program that enables Internet users to trade messages in real time, simulating a conversation.
Irregular Movement	The random movement of time series, which is not explained by other components. In this sense it is a residual of other components.
ISAR Systems	Objectives, Types, Operations and Design
ISCII	Indian Standard Code for Character Interchange.
ISDN	Integrated Services Digital Network is a system of digital phone connections that allows voice and data. There are two basic types of ISDN service.
ISO	International Organisation for Standardisation was established in 1947 as a worldwide federation of national standards bodies from some 130 countries.

ISO-2709	An international standard for bibliographic information interchange on magnetic tape, developed in 1981.
ISP	Internet Service Provider, a company that provides access to the Internet. Typically these service providers also offer web hosting services to their users.
Item Entry System	Types of post coordinate indexing system in which items are posted on the term.
Iterative search	Searches of information service provider that get modified in the light of the interaction with users reaction to the search results.
ITRC	Indian Toxicological Research Centre.
Jacket	A polyester flap of size 105 x 148 mm having channels of 16 mm/35 mm size for keeping microfilm strips.
Jargon	Every profession has a specialized language which conveys ft is and concepts quickly and efficiently among the group.
Java	Developed by Sun Microsystems, Java is a programming language that is specifically designed for writing programs.
JavaScript	JavaScript is a scripting language from Netscape Java and JavaScript are not the same?
JCC	J-Gate Custom Content.
JCCC	J-Gate Custom Content for Consortium.
J-Gate	Journal Gate way Service from Informatics, India Pvt. Ltd., Bangalore.
Journal	Acts as an intermediate link in the evolution of Information.
Judgment Sampling	In this sampling procedure the selection of sample is based on the researcher's judgment.
Jughead	Jughead is a computer program that searches a particular Gopher site.
Justified	A technical term in printing. A page of print that is arranged in such a way that both the left hand and right hand edges are straight.
Kashghar	Town and Caravan Centre in the West Sinkiang

	Province of China, near the edge of Takla Makan Desert.
KBS	Knowledge Based Systems, also known as Expert System and Knowledge Based Computer Systems (KBCS).
Kettle Stitch	A stitch made at the head and tail of the book to fasten one section to another when a book is being sewed.
Keyword	Technically, a significant word / term taken from the text of a document (see also Descriptor).
Keyword Indexing	An indexing system based on the usage of natural language terminology for deriving the index entries.
Keyword Search	Searching databases on the topic of a keyword entered by the searcher.
Knowledge	Knowledge is an organized set of statements of ideas, presenting a reasoned. judgment or an experimental result.
Knowledge Base	A knowledge base is an expert system's database of knowledge about a particular subject.
Knowledge Engineering	Techniques of building knowledge into expert systems. That is understanding knowledge in specific domains.
Knowledge Mediators	Persons or libraries who provide users with insight into the existing body of knowledge.
Knowledge Representation	Method of codifying knowledge to enable a computer to store, process and to draw inference from the codified knowledge.
KOHA	An open source library management software available for downloading from Internet at no cost.
KQML	Knowledge Query and Management Language.
Label	Any paper, plastic, etc. permanently affixed to a physical carrier or information printed or embossed.
Laissez-faire Leadership	A leadership style in which the leader exercises very little control or influence over group

	members.
Lamination	Protecting and strengthening paper by covering one or both sides with transparent tissue paper.
LAN	A network workstations that are linked together within a limited geographical areas.
Language (HTML)	Mints on the World Wide Web. HTML text files contain content that is rendered on a computer screen.
Language	Difference in linguistic behaviour because of differences in language retaining the original meaning.
Laser	It is an acronym, the expanded form being light amplification by stimulated emission of radiation.
Lay Readers	Readers who have just a commonsense knowledge of a subject or profession.
Laying Press	Also known as 'Cutting Press', on which the edges of the bond volume are trimmed.
Learning	An intelligent attribute that signifies some form of learning.
Lexicographer	A writer or compiler of a dictionary. [RHD].
Libertarianism	Principles or doctrines of the freedom of will.
Library	Anybody which is responsible for library.
Library and Information Professionals	Professionals engaged in library and information science activities as a paid profession.
Library Automation	Library automation is the mechanization of housekeeping operations and information handling activities.
Library Board	The committee responsible for the control of an American library system.
Library Committee	The committee set up for the governance of the library.
Library Consortia	Libraries and publishers coming together for mutual benefit and enabling collaborative acquisition of e-documents to a group of libraries.
Library Cooperation	Two or more libraries working together to achieve their goals providing effective service to

	their users.
Library Governing Body	Person or a collective body of persons empowered by law to act on behalf of the library concerned.
Library History	Historical research conducted in the field of library and information science.
Library Housekeeping	A group of basic routine operations related to acquiring, preparing, circulating and preserving the library documents for their maximum use.
Library Management	A software package used for the carrying out the Software functions and services performed by libraries.
Library Networks	Two or more libraries connected together through telecommunication links for effective sharing of resources overcoming the barriers of geographical distances.
Life Expectancy (LE)	The number of years a microfilm, an optical disc etc. is expected to be useful.
Light emitting diode (LED)	A low-cost optical source that produces light when electric current is applied to it.
Linear Programming	A mathematical technique that attempts to allocate limited or scarce resources among competing demands in an optimum way.
Linguistic Features of language	Phonetics (Sounds), syntax (grammar) and lexis (vocabulary) of a of language.
Link	The anchor tag (<A>) is used to define both anchors and links.
Link Text	The rendered text content of a link.
Links	Special symbols used to group all the related concepts in a document separately for the elimination of false drops.
Linotype	A typesetting machine, generally used by press and big industrial houses.
Linux	A free Unix-type operating system originally created by Linus Torvalds with the assistance of developers around the world.
Listserv	A mailing list program for communicating with other people who have subscribed to the same

	list.
Lithography	The process of printing from a flat metal surface treated.
Liturgical Works	Fixed form of public worship used in churches.
Log File	A special file maintained by a Database Management System contains information about all updates to a database.
Logical Progression	Logical sequence of things taking place.
Look Smart	A website directory that has commercial search listings.
Low-Technique Readers	Readers who have a smattering knowledge of a subject or profession.
Lycos	One of the large and popular search engines, Lycos appears to be moving towards becoming a directory for some search results.
Machine Direction of Paper	In the process of manufacturing machine-made paper, the fibers mostly get set along the direction in which the pulp runs.
Machine language	A binary type low-level language consisting of 1s and 0s that the computer can run directly.
Mailing Listor	Also sometimes called a 'discussion list' or 'listserv', a Listserv mailing list is a group of e-mail users.
Main Entry	The entry determined by AACR2 to be the primary access point for the item.
Man –Machine: Chart	These are designed to analyze the work relationships between a man and one or more machines.
Management	Management is the process of leading and directing all or part of an organisation, often a business, through the deployment.
Management by Objectives	It is the formal procedure where a management pair periodically reaches mutual agreements to achieve specific goal or objectives of an organization.
Management Functions	The major components of a manager's job. They include planning, organization, motivating and controlling.

Management Information System	It is a system that provides all levels of management with all the relevant information.
Management Information Systems (MIS)	A system designed to use all" data collected by an organisation to provide management with the information needed for decision making.
Management Principles	Guides for managerial action. They are fundamental truths of organisation and management.
Manuals	A handbook published by an organisation giving practical step by step instructions on how to do a particular job; can be used to impart training on the job.
Manuscript	A handwritten or typed text awaiting printing and publication.
Manuscript Hieroglyphics	Egyptians developed a word-syllabic writing, known as hieroglyphic, about 3000 BC. It is a kind of picture writing.
MARC	A machine-readable catalogue for the purpose of communicating bibliographic information to large number of libraries.
MARC Cataloguing	The process of recording bibliographic information about an item and then coding that information for the machine.
MARC Format	A bibliographic record format that has been devised for the MARC project.
Margin of Error	Degree of deviation of sample from being a true representative of a population drawn by random sampling.
Marketing Research	It aims at testing, identifying and measuring the market in order to provide better and improved services.
Markup Language	For describing information. Information in SGML (SGML) is structured like a database, supporting rendering in and conversion between.
Mass Communication	Information communicated to a large audience.
Mass Media	Information communicated to a large audience

	using a variety of ICTs and digital technologies with great effect.
Master Database	A main file of information that acts as the core database. Entries made once in the master file are available for data entry work in related files.
Matric Organisation	Organisation dealing with multi products or well defined projects, where the division of work and responsibility is organized on the basis of different products and projects.
Matter	Written material prepared for printing.
Mechanical Wood	Cheap paper made by grinding raw wood into pulp (newsprint). All impurities and acid substances remain in the paper.
Mechanics	Mechanical or functional details that have to be attended to in the production of a text i.e. details of punctuation.
Media	The physical media that carry messages or contents of information.
Media Persons	Specialists and experts of different categories functioning and operating in mass media communication.
Median	In a set of observations, it is the value of the middlemost item when they are arranged in order of magnitude.
Message	An informational statement that describes the state of an object in the universe.
Meta Document	An instrument record of natural and social phenomena made directly unmediated by the human mind.
Meta Resources	Meta resource is a database of Internet resource descriptions that is made accessible through a structured and/or unstructured network service.
Meta Search Engine	A search engine that simultaneously searches multiple search engines in response to a query.
Meta tag	The HTML element used to demarcate metadata on a Web page.
Metadata	Data about data, or information known about the image in order to provide access to the image.

Metadata Harvesting	A technique for extracting metadata from individual repositories and collecting it in a central catalogue to facilitate search inter-operability.
Metadata Schema	A metadata element set and rules for using it.
Metadata	MARC21-856 Field, Dublin Core, TEI.
Meta search	A search service that sends keywords to several search services at the same time.
Meta-search Engines	Also sometimes called 'mete-crawlers' and 'multi-search engines', these allow users to search several search facilities once at the same time.
Method of Least Squares	When a polynomial function is fitted to the time series, the method of least squares requires that the parameters of the function.
MHRD	Ministry of Human Resources Development, Government of India.
Micro Facsimile	A copy of an original reproduced in micro size.
Micro card	An opaque microform of size 3"x5".
Microfiche	A transparent microform, usually of size 105 mm x 148 mm having rows of reduced images.
Microfilm	Photographic film used to store text and still images in greatly reduced form, intended for use with a special viewer or reader.
Microlex	An opaque card of 6.5"x8.5" size capable of storing about 200 reduced images on one side.
Micro-opaque	The microform through which light cannot pass through.
Microprint	An opaque card larger than microcard having a size of 6"x9" and consists of 100 images with an eye legible bibliographic entry.
Micropublisher	A publisher that brings out publications in microforms.
Microsoft Outlook Express	It is a component of Internet Explorer that integrates an e-mail and newsgroup services.
Micro-transparency	The microform through which light can be transmitted.
Mid-value	It is the average value of two class limits. It falls just in the middle of a class.

Mildew	Destructive growth of minute fungi on paper, leather etc., exposed to warm, damp climate.
Milieu, Social	Refers to the man's social environment or surroundings.
Miniaturisation	A copy of the document which is greatly reduced and usually read or reproduced by means of optical aids.
Mitring	A joint at 45 as in the leather or the inside of the boards.
Mixed Design	A special design where one factor is between and the other is within.
Mixed Readers	Composite readers with various degree of specialization in a discipline or profession but having a common interest in a particular subject.
Mobile Agents	Agents are capable of moving from machine to machine in a heterogeneous network environment and executing themselves on any machine.
Mode	In a set of observations, it is the value which occurs with maximum frequency.
Model Act	A design of the act to be followed.
Modem	Modulator / demodulator, a device that allows computers to communicate over telephone lines by converting digital signals to analogue.
Modulation	Embedding base signals in high frequency carriers.
Module	Functions specific to a particular system capability such as the online public access catalog, cataloging.
Moisture	Something which makes slightly wet, liquid at a given relative humidity and temperature.
Monitoring Team	It refers to experts from outside the organisation specially selected for guiding, monitoring and controlling certain activities or processes.
Monotype	A typesetting machine generally used by the press and big publishing houses.
Morpholine	An organic amononia-based solvent used by

	Barrow Laboratories for mass deacidification.
Motion Study	It determines precisely what steps a job.
Motivation	An intense desire to achieve something, and willingness to work hard in order to succeed.
Mould	Fine furry growth of fungi that forms on old food or on objects left in moist warm air.
Moulds	Fine furry growth of fungi that forms on old food or on object left in the moist warm air.
Mouse Movements	The mouse points to the location of the desired item on the screen with the help of a cursor called mouse pointer.
Multilingual data	Data in more than one language in the same document or file.
Multimedia	Computer systems dcsignedlto capture. store, process. retrieve, display and playback.
Multiple Readers	More or less similar to mixed readers.
Multiplexing	Sending more than one information signal on the same communication medium.
Multistage Sampling	The sample selection is done in a number of stages. Parameter : It is a measure of some characteristic of the population.
My Computer	My Computer gives a quick overview of all the files and programs available in the system.
My Documents	It gives a quick overview of all the documents saved in the system. Any document that is saved gets into My Documents folder automatically.
Nadir	The lowest point on the spiral of scientific method where the problem for research is identified and formally formulated.
National Academic Depository (NAD)	The Union Cabinet has approved establishing a digital depository of academic awards to be known as National Academic Depository (NAD) on the pattern of securities depository in its meeting held on 27th October, 2016.
Natural Language	It refers to the area that attempts to make the Processing (NLP) computer understand natural language.
Navigation Bar	A navigation bar is a collection of links to most

	important parts of a document or site.
Navigation Mechanism	A navigation mechanism is any means by which a user can navigate a page or site.
Navigational	Ability to choose destinations, select route, and plan Autonomy itinerary autonomously.
Navigators	Finding your way around in cyberspace.
NBRI	National Botanical Research Institute
NDLTD	The Networked Digital Library of Theses and Dissertations (NDLTD) is an international organisation dedicated to promotion and dissemination of electronic theses and dissertations.
Neo-Conventional Documents	The "Standards, specifications, patents, data of properties in natural sciences and their applications, reaction formulae in chemistry, differential clinical data in medicine.
Nested	An element that is entirely contained within another element. For example, the phrase 'the quick brown fox' contains a bold element (the word 'quick') nested within an italic element.
Netscape Navigator	A multimedia browser for accessing information which is available via the WWW.
Network	An interconnection of three or more communicating entities or A system of computers interconnected by telephone wires or other means in order to share information.
Network Analysis	It helps in designing, planning, coordinating, controlling and in decision making in order to accomplish a project economically in the minimum available time with the limited available resources.
Network Reassembling	The process of assembling packets or cells to reconstruct the original message at the destination.
Newsletters	Newsletters are publications issued by organisations, often simple in format and crisp in style, they provide speedy information for a definite public (audience).
NISCAIR	National Institute of Science Communication

	and Information Resources (formerly INSDOC).
Node	Any device connected to a computer network. Nodes can be computers, or any network appliances.
Noise	Disturbance in a communication system.
Noise factor	The proportion of retrieved items those are not relevant. This factor is considered as the complement of the precision ratio.
Nominal Scale	Nominal measurement consists of assigning items to groups or categories.
Nominal Variable	Such a variable takes qualitative values and do not have any ordering relationships among them.
Nominated Member	Appointed or named or designated for the position, ordinarily Govts.
Non-book Media	The generic term used for different types of non-paper media such as magnetic media, optical media, film media etc.
Non-Conventional Documents	Micro reproduction of conventional documents; audio; visual; and audio-visual records.
Non-Documentary	Sources that are not in the form of documents, e.g. Sources organizations, persons.
Normal Equations	A set of simultaneous equations derived in the application of the least squares method, for example in regression analysis.
Normalisation	The process of creating a well-behaved set of tables to efficiently store data, minimize redundancy and ensure data integrity.
Novelty ratio	The proportion of relevant documents retrieved in a search that are new to the requester, that is, brought to his attention for the first time by the search.
Null Hypothesis	Hypothesis, that there is no evidence that the treatment has an effect.
OAI	Open Access Initiative.
Object	Anything in the creation: animate, inanimate etc.
Object-Oriented	It is based on object oriented data model

	defined by Database Kim in 1991. In this Management System and sharable objects supporting object oriented principles.
Observation	A recording of a single datum.
Octavo	A full sheet of paper folded three times to give 16 pages.
ODBC	Stands for Open Data Base Connectivity. ODBC is a de facto standard programming interface developed by Microsoft for accessing a database.
Omission factor	The proportion of non-relevant items retrieved over the total number of non-retrieved items in the collection.
ONIX	Online Information Exchange International.
On-line	Using the devices and peripherals, which are interacting directly and simultaneously with a computer central processing unit.
Online Catalogue	The catalogue is stored in machine-readable form and accessed online by the library clientele by employing user friendly software.
Online Search Services	Information providers or database producers who provide databases to be accessed in an online mode.
Ontology	The branch of metaphysics that studies the nature of existence.
OPAC	The OPAC is an online database of materials held by a library or group of libraries. OPAC is the gateway to library's collection.
Opaque Microcopy	A microcopy made on opaque, or non-transparent, material, usually paper or card.
Open Access	A library system where readers are admitted to the shelves.
Open Directory	A directory project run by thousands of volunteer editors.
Open Ended Questions	They are also called unstructured questions. In such questions respondents express their views freely.
Open Source Software	Open source software is typically created and maintained by developers crossing institutional

	and national boundaries, collaborating.
Open System	A system that interact with its environment.
Open-end Class	A class in which one of the limits is not specified.
Operations Research	It is the application of mathematical models that permit comparisons of alternative courses of action.
Optical Character	The OCR refers to the process of scanning text using a Recognization (OCR) scanning device from a printed page into an image and translates it into a computer processible format.
Optical Devices	Making a copy of a document on photographic material in the same scale or one different from the original.
Optical Disc	A plastic disc that is "written" (encoded) and "read" using a laser optical device. It can store digital data as tiny pits etched in the surface.
Optical Fiber	A thin glass or plastic fibre used to carry data in the form of light waves.
Oral Communication	Audio presentation of information.
Oral Form of Inf.	Information communicated orally.
Ordinal scale	Measurements with ordinal scales are ordered in the sense that higher numbers represent higher values.
Organisation. ASTINFO	Regional Network for Exchange of Information and Experience in Science and Technology in Asia and the Pacific – a UNESCO sponsored regional programme.
Organizing Classification	It refers to the categorization of concepts and their organsation on the basis of genus-species, whole-part, and other inter-facet relationships.
Orientation	Formal orientation of the library to the user through direct and indirect method.
Origins	They may be written by content providers, created by users, or built into user agents.
OSI	Stands for Open Systems Interconnection. OSI is a seven-layer architecture model for communications systems developed by the ISO

	for the interconnection of data communications systems.
Output Devices	A device used for transferring data from internal storage of a computer to an external device or user.
Overt Observation	In this type of observation the participants are aware that they are being observed.
Oxidation	A chemical reaction between oxygen and another substance, causing the original substance to have its properties altered.
Packet switching	A switching technique in which large size data is broken as packets and transferred across networks.
Palaeography	Ancient modes of writing, study of ancient modes of hand writing.
Pamphlet	A non-periodical publication of atleast five but not more than 49 pages, exclusive of the cover pages. (General Conference of Unesco, 1964).
Paradigm	It is defined as a pattern or model.
Parameter	It is a measure of some characteristic of the population.
Para-Professional	A person without professional training to whom a particular aspect of a professional task is delegated.
Parser	A computational process that takes individual sentences or concerned texts and converts them to some representational structure useful for further processing.
Parsing	It refers to the use syntax to determine the functions of words in the input sentences in order to create a data structure that can be used to get at the meaning of the sentence.
Participant Observation	Observation where the observer is part of the observant He participates in all the activities of the group while observing them.
Participative Management	A style of management in which the employees take appropriate part in every activity of the organisation.
Paste-down	The half of the fly leaf or end paper which is

	pasted down to thecover board.
Patent	A publication, issued by such an office, which gives details of designs and processes.
Pay-per-view	A method by which non-subscribers can download specific articles (fulltext) of their interest by paying specified charges per article.
Peers	Groups of people of similar status in an organisation.
Penumbra	Partly shaded area around the shadow of an opaque object, referring the related areas of information to get additional information relevant to a query.
Performance Criterion	Standard for judging performance.
Performance Curve	A performance curve is nothing but a line representing graphically a series of variable performance points in terms of recall and precision.
Performance Evaluation	It helps to assess how. well a system or service is working with respect to some predefined measures.
Performance Measurement	It means investigating and measuring how well an operational system meet the needs of its users.
Permanent virtual	A virtual circuit assigned on a long-term basis.
Perquisites	Payments, emoluments or other benefits gained by a public official beyond his regular salary while acting in his official capacity.
Personal Interview	It is a face – to face interaction between researcher and respondent.
Personal System of Information (PSI)	Individual user's profile for modulated and planned independent study.
Personnel	The total human resources of an organization.
Perspective	Characterizes any approach which attempts to lay down rules of correctness as to how language should be used, with an aim to preserve imagined standards.
PERT	Program Evaluation and Review Technique –a

	network analysis technique.
Phatic	Refers to language used for establishing or maintaining.
Phenomenon	Fact or occurrence (Phenomena is the plural form).
Phonetic Writing	It is a word-syllabic system of writing. The Sumerians devised a fully developed form of it around 3000 BC.
Photodetector	A device that accepts light as input and produces electric current as output.
Phrase searching	Phrase searching retrieves only documents with the exact combination of words and in the exact order.
Phythmic	The quality of happening at regular periods of time.
Pictorial Form of Information	Information communicated through pictures instead of alphabets and symbols.
Pie Chart	It is a circle sub-divided into components to present proportion of different constituent parts of a total.
Planned Change	Systematic, deliberate change in the way part or all of an organisation functions.
Planning	Determining the direction of a business by establishing objectives and by designing and implementing the strategies necessary to achieve those objectives.
Plans	Document giving a complete blue print for executing an activity.
Plate	A plate is a photograph or an illustration that is printed anywhere in the book except facing the title page. Normally, a plate covers the whole page.
Plug-Ins	Software programs that enhance other programs or applications on your computer.
Point	Unit of measurement of type-size (1 inch = 72 prints) in printing; 6-point is small and 18-point is large print.
Pointer	A logical or physical address of a piece of data.
Pointing	Pointing refers to the positioning of the mouse

	pointer at a specific location on the screen.
Population	It is the entire collection of units of a specified type in a given place and at a particular point of time.
Portable Document	Portable Document Format is a type of formatting that enables Format (PDF) files to be viewed on a variety computers regardless of the program originally used to create them.
Portrait	A portrait is a painting, drawing, etc. usually of the face of a person.
Post - Print	A scientific paper after peer review and editorial changes.
Post Coordinate Indexing	Component terms in a compound subject are kept separately uncoordinated by the indexer.
PostScript	A page description language developed and marketed by Adobe Systems. PostScript can be used by a wide variety of computers and printers.
Pragmatic information	Where informational value of a message is assessed based on a given context. Also known as contextual information.
Precision	A standard measure of IR performance, precision is defined as the number of relevant documents retrieved divided by the total number of documents retrieved.
Pre-coordinate Indexing	The indexer carries out Coordination of component terms in a compound subject at the time of indexing by following the syntactical rules of a given indexing language.
Pre-print	The version of a scientific paper sent to publisher for publication.
Preprints	Preprints most often refer to manuscripts that have not yet been published, but may have been reviewed.
Presentation Materials	Textual and visual materials that supplement and complement oral presentations.
Pretesting	Before finalizing the questions in the questionnaire it is circulated to a sample for their opinion and suggestions.

Primary Colour	Colours that are basis for all other colour combinations. Primary colours are red, green and blue (RGB).
Primary Key	A column or a set of columns that identify a particular row in a table.
Primary Sources	Sources that carry original contributions, information that is appearing for the first time, etc. These are the base for secondary sources.
Primary Term	A term figuring in the source article title and appears as the main entry in the Permuterm Subject Index.
Principle of Osmosis	When a library switches over to a new scheme of classification or to a new catalogue code the principle of osmosis suggests a smooth
Printed Form of Information	Information printed on a medium like paper.
Private Knowledge	The knowledge of the mind of an individual and as such is available to him/ her or through him/her to others, if communicated.
Problem	A description of the problem you shall study in your research work.
Process	One of the fundamental categories propounded by Kaiser, which includes mode of treatment of the subject by the author.
Process States	Different states in which an active agent program may exist.
Prodigy	Prodigy is one of the providers of online services in USA. In addition to providing access to the Internet and World Wide Web.
Product Co-term	A term figuring in the source article title and subordinated to a primary term in the Permuterm Subject Index.
Productivity	Relationship between input and output of an organization. Input being measured in men, machines, materials and money, and output in products and services.
Profession	A paid occupation, especially one involving training.
Professional	A person engaged in an activity as a paid

	occupation rather than as an amateur.
Professional Services	Library and information services that need writing skills.
Professional Writings	Writings that deal with professional services.
Profiling	User profile (individual, group/community) of information needs in conceptual terms.
Program Indexing	Computer software used to order things; frequently used to refer to software that alphabetizes some or all of the terms in one or more electronic documents.
Programmes	Pressure of user demands. The resources may be physical or intellectual.
Promotion	Advancement or encouragement on behalf of some cause, product, service or organisation.
Promotional Role	Activities related to raise the capacity of the library in providing services to its users.
Proposals	Technical writings that deal with a formal offer of undertaking any activity.
Protocol	A protocol is a standardized means of communication among machines across a network.
Proximity Operator	A set of operators to combine search terms that permit the searcher to specify the context in which a search term should occur.
Proximity Searching	Searching for terms that occur within a specified number of words in the text.
Proxy server	A proxy server is a server that acts as an intermediary between a computer and the Internet.
Prussian Instructions	The German cataloguing rules of an English translation was published by the University of Michigan Press in 1938.
PSTN	Short for Public Switched Telephone Network, this is the standard telephone service that most homes use. It is also referred to as POTS, or Plain Old Telephone Service.
Psychiatrist	A doctor trained in the study and treatment of diseases of the mind.

Purist	One who insists on preserving what she/he considers the 'correct' form of language, and is against language variation and language change.
PURL	Persistent Uniform Resource Locator is an approach to the URL permanence problem proposed by OCLC.
Planning-Programming-Budgeting System (PPBS)	The PPBS method is to set certain major objectives, to define programmes essential to these goals. (United States Department of Defence) (1961).
Quadrant	One of the four equal sectors or areas into which the spiral of scientific method is divided.
Quality	The dictionary definition of `Quality' of a person or a thing is a characteristic, innate or acquired, etc.
Quality Assurance	QA is the method of and a philosophy for achieving better quality.
Quality Circles	A Quality Circle is a small group of between three and twelve people who do the same, or similar work.
Quality Control	QC is a process to determine how the technological, human, information and financial resources are being used effectively to get the best results.
Quality Improvement	Adding value to information products and services using appropriate performance standards.
Quality of Indexing	The ability to retrieve what is wanted and to avoid what is not wanted.
Quarto	A full sheet of paper folded twice to give 8 pages.
Query	A string of words that characterizes the information that the user seeks.
Questionnaire	A formal and structured list of questions prepared by researcher to be asked.
Quota Sampling	In this sampling procedure the samples are selected on the basis of some parameters such as age, gender, geographical region, education,

	income, religion, etc.
Quotation	Group of words taken from a book, play, speech etc. and used again by persons other than the original author.
RAID	Redundant Array of Independent Disks. A disk drive system that consists of multiple drives with independent controllers.
Random Sample	A sample drawn by probability technique in which every element of population has equal and independent chance of inclusion in the sample.
Random Sampling	It is a procedure where every member of the population has a definite chance or probability of being selected in the sample. It is also called probability sampling.
Randomization	A tool used to establish internal variability.
Random sampling could be of many types	Simple random sampling, systematic random sampling and stratified random.
Range	It is the difference between the largest and the smallest observations of a given set of data.
Rank Order Scale	Respondents are asked to rank all items according to some specified order.
Rank-and-file	Placement of staff in an ascending or descending order according to importance.
Rare Book	A book of value, which is scarce and not easily available.
Ratio scale	Ratio scales are like interval scales except they have true zero points. Ratio variables are very similar to interval variables.
Raw Data	Data, in machine-sensible form or otherwise, which has not been processed.
Readability of	Features of a book which makes it accessible/difficult.
Reader	Individual or a group of individuals who have potential for being exposed to and using an information product or service.
reader a Book Syllable	Part of a word that contains a single vowel-sound and that is pronounced as a unit.

Reader Analysis	Analyzing a target group with reference to a writing situation. A reader who is well-versed in any discipline or profession.
Recall	A measure to check how well a system performs at yielding up all relevant items within it.
Recipient	The ultimate receiver of information who may also generate or create information.
Recipient-centered	Where informational value of a message is assessed based on the recipient's perception of the meaning. Also called user-centered.
Record	A collection of fields that form a logically related and discrete unit of information.
Recycle Bin	It keeps all deleted files, to retrieve them later.
Redundancy	Use of more words than are necessary to convey an idea or thought.
Reference Interview	That part of the reference process in which the inquirer and the searcher interact to stabilize the enquiry.
Reference Query	Any request by a library user for information or assistance in locating information.
Reference Service	It is a process of answering questions or satisfying specific, Process recurrent information needs.
Referral Specialist	A person or a group who acts as a middleman to link the user with the information sources.
Register	Variety of languages defined according to their use in situations, e.g., a register of scientific, religious, formal English.
Regression	It is a statistical measure of the average relationship between two or more variables in terms of the original units of the data.
Relation	A relation is a table.
Relational Database	Relational Database Management System is based on Management System the concept of relational data model.
Relational Indexing	The identification of the relationship between each pair of terms of a given subject statement and representation of those relations by

	relational operators.
Relational Operators	Special symbols used to link the isolates in Relational Indexing to create analects.
Relationship	An association between two or more entities.
Relative Frequency	It is frequency distribution where the frequency of Distribution each value is expressed as a fraction or a percentage of the total number of observations.
Relative Humidity	The quantity of water vapour in the air relative to the temperature of the atmosphere.
Relative Index	An index showing various aspects of an idea and its relationship with other ideas.
Release	A minor upgrade in a software product. It is usually indicated by a change in number after the decimal point such as 3.0, 3.1, 3.11, etc.
Relevance	An abstract measure of how well a document satisfies the user's information need. Ideally, system should retrieve all of the relevant documents.
Relevancy Ranking	The process of displaying search results in an order based on an algorithm that considers the number of occurrences of the search term(s) in the documents.
Reliable communication	Achieving error-free communication by the use of coding techniques.
Remote Access	OPAC is an online catalog of a library collection that is available to the public. Today most libraries make their OPAC publicly accessible via the Web.
Repeater	A device used in microwave radio communication which filters noise from the incoming signal, amplifies and retransmits the signal to the next station at the same frequency.
Reports	A special type of publication with a given format and structure use to communicate facts, ideas, results of research, etc.
Repository	A book store belonging to one library system, or a number of co-operative library systems prepared to inter-lend the books deposited

	therein.
Reprographer	A person who reproduces or duplicates printed documents, written material, drawings, designs, etc.
Reprography	The reproduction in facsimile of documents of all kinds by any process using light, heat or electric variation – photocopies, micro-copies, blue prints, electro-copies, thermo-copies, etc.
Research	Systematic inquiry into a subject in order to discover or revise facts, theories, etc.
Research Design	A plan of action or a blueprint.
Research Library	RLG is an international not-for-profit membership Group (RLG) organisation of libraries, museums.
Research Plan	The blue print of your research that states everything from the title to the limitations of your study.
Resequencing	The process of arranging the packets in proper order when they arrive out of sequence at the destination.
Resolution	Resolution refers to the number of pixels contained on a display monitor, printers and bit-mapped graphic images.
Resolution factor	The proportion of total items retrieved over a total number of items in the collection.
Resource Description	A generic framework for describing and interchanging metadata on Framework (RDF) the Internet.
Resource Guides	The JISC is establishing posts known as Resource Guides in a number of subject areas.
Resource Sharing	It denotes a mode of opefation whereby resources and services are shared in common by a number of libraries.
Response Rate	The number of respondents returned the filled in questionnaire.
Retrieval (Z39.50)	Application Service Definition and Protocol Specification" and ANSI/NISO Z39.50-1995.
Retrieval Status Values	In retrieval process, the query description and (RSVs) document descriptions are matched and

	a score is generated for every document pair.
Retrospective Conversion	The conversion of previously catalogued library materials to machine-readable form.
Review	Primary literature analyzed, synthesized and integrated ii) Primary literature further compacted and repackaged for specific category of users.
Rexene	A fabric based product. Thick and strong fabric is given a thick surface coating, and then calendared to create grains on the surface.
RFID	RFID stands for Radio Frequency Identification. RFID system comprises three components: a tag, a reader and an antenna.
RH	Relative humidity.
Rhetoric	The art of speaking or writing that sounds fine.
Right	Motivation or sense of purpose of the communicator, as well as Perspective that of audience.
Roboform	Example of software that helps in automatically filling forms while surfing the net.
Robot	Any browser program which follows hypertext links and accesses web pages but is not directly under human control.
Role	A symbol attached to the index term to indicate the context in which the term has been used.
Role Operators	These refer to a set of notations, which specifies the grammatical role or function of the term which follows the operators and which regulates the order of the terms in an input string in PRECIS.
Roll Microfilm	The commonly used microform, available in 16mm, 35mm, 70mm and 105mm sizes. These are usually rolled in spools, cassettes and cartridges and hence the nomenclature.
Rosetta Stone	It is a piece of ancient Egyptian Stone, bearing inscriptions. It is now preserved in the British Museum. It was discovered in 1799 AD.
Reeslieaabrcilhity Process	The measure of being able to measure the variables with the same accuracy at different

	times under similar conditions refer to reliability.
RRL	Regional Research Laboratory.
RSS	Really Simple Syndication; A system of getting the latest revised version of a web page automatically using pull technology.
RSS Aggregator	A software program needed to download RSS feeds. It is special type of news fetcher-cum-browser.
RSS Feed	An XML file in a website that offers its readers the facility of downloading latest revised version of a page or news items automatically.
Sample	It is a sub-set of the population. Therefore, it is a collection of some units from the population.
Sampling Distribution	It is the relative frequency or probability distribution of the values of a statistic when the number of samples tends to infinity.
Sampling Error	In the sampling method, we try to approximate some feature of a given population from a sample drawn from it.
Save File Formats	PDF (.pdf) or XPS (.xps), Rich Text Format (.rtf), Word 97-2003 (.doc), Web Page (.htm or .html).
Scaling Technique	A finite sample of concepts or items is ordered along a continuum.
Scanner	A scanner is an 'input device that transfers information from a piece of paper in to a computer.
Schema	An overall conceptual or logical view of the relationships between the data in a database.
Scientific	A method of research in which a problem is identified, relevant Method data gathered, hypothesis formulated and the hypothesis empirically tested.
Scientific Management	A style of management in which scientific management principles are applied to production, control, distribution and other activities in an organisation.
Scientific Method	Any objective, transparent and repeatable method based on direct and systematic

	observation of phenomena to study cause-effect relation between two or more variables.
Scopus	A fulltext Science Only Service started by Elsevier in late 2004.
Scribe	A person who serves as a penman or copyist, especially one who in former times made copies of manuscripts.
SDI	Selective Dissemination of Information.
Seamless Integration	Integration of text, image and sound in a digital information environment without any binding chord fastening each form.
Search Engine	A searchable database of Internet files collected by a computer program (called a wanderer, crawler, robot, worm, and spider.
Search Language	An artificial language used to construct search statements that can be input to an IRS.
Search Strategy	A conceptual schema developed to locate information from a file.
Search Term	A Search Term is an expression, a sequence of signs, letters and/or figures relevant to a specific query.
Seasonal Variation	Periodical movement where the period is not longer than one year.
Secondary Form of Information	Information generated from primary information e.g. an abstract.
Secondary Sources	Sources that are based on the material published in the primary sources.
Section	A sheet of paper consisting generally of 4, 8 or 16 leaves folded and ready to be incorporated in the main body of the book, also called *'signature'* or *form.*
Secular Trend	The smooth, regular and long-term movement of a time series over a period of time.
Semantic	Meaning of words and their relationships.
Semantic factoring	Involves the analysis of a word into largest number of ideas implied.
Semantic information	Where informational value of a message is assessed by the amount of substantive information contained in it without regard to

	the context, sender or recipient.
Semantic Net	A directed graph in which nodes represent entities and arcs entities.
Semantic Web	The term Semantic Web of the current Web in which information is given well-defined meaning, better enabling computers and people to work in cooperation.
Semantics	Concerns the meaning conveyed by sentences.
Sensitized Material	Material used in documentary reproduction which is coated with an emulsion sensitive to light or heat as used in a thermo graphic process.
Sequential Access	Access that takes records in order, looking at the first, then the next, and so on. Access Method.
Serendipity	Tile faculty of making desirable discoveries by accident.
Serrated	The roughened surface having rows of small projections like teeth of saw.
Server	A program running on an Internet site that makes the web pages at that site available to browsers throughout the Internet.
Sewing Frame	It consists of a bed with two uprights and a cross bar which can be raised or lowered as required. The volume to be bound is set on the bed for sewing.
SGML	Standard Generalized Markup Language – a standard for describing markup languages. A mark-up language alters the presentation of the content of a document.
Shielded Twisted Pair	Shielded pair of wires that are twisted.
Signal	A time varying electrical, optical or electromagnetic quantity representing information, speech, video, etc.
Signalling	Indicative or control signals exchanged between a subscriber and a switching node or between two switching nodes.
Signature	A sheet of paper consisting generally of 4, 8 or

	16 leaves folded and ready to be incorporated in the main body of the book. Also known as 'Section'.
Significance Level	There may be certain samples where population mean would not remain within the confidence interval around sample mean.
Silk Chiffon	Finely woven silk. It is used for the repair of fragile papers, hardly discernible when pasted down.
Simple and Sub-divided Bar	In the case of simple bar diagram only one diagram variable can be presented.
Simple Random Sampling	This is the basic sampling procedure where all units in the population have an equal chance of being included in the sample.
Simplified Form of Information	Information presented replacing the jargons, difficult words and long
Site	Internet website.
Site Map	A site map provides a global view of the organization of a page or site.
Sizing	A gelatinous solution used in coating and glazing paper surface.
SLIP/PPP	Serial Line Internet Protocol / Point-to-Point Protocol. Allows a computer with a modem to connect to the Internet using TCP/IP.
Slips	The ends of the tape on which the book is stitched, that are attached to the board. Also known as 'back'.
SMTP	Stands for Simple Mail Transport Protocol. The main protocol used to send electronic mail on the Internet.
SMTP/UUCP	Simple Mail Transfer Protocol/ Unix to Unix Copy
Snowball Sampling	It relies on referrals from initial sampling units to generate additional sampling units.
Social Knowledge	The knowledge possessed collectively by a society or a social system and supposed
Social Research	Large scale social surveys from a large number of cases to discover the distribution and interrelationships of social and attitudinal

	variables.
Sociology of Knowledge	The science or study of the origin, development, organisation and functioning of human society.
Software	Documenting computer programs, procedures, rules
Software Agent	A computer program that carries out tasks on behalf of another entity.
Sole Agent	A book-supplier who will supply reading materials on all subjects to a library.
SOUL	SOUL stands for Software for University Libraries. It is a library automation software package developed by INFLIBNET, Ahmadabad.
Source	The mode of communicating messages through signs, symbols, texts or graphics.
Source Article Title	The title of the source article covered by the Source Index of the Science Citation Index.
Source coding	Coding of source messages to achieve efficiency in information communication.
Source entropy	Average information content of a message from the source.
Source Item	A document, i.e., a research paper, a review paper, a short communication, etc. that has the potentiality of being cited.
Sources of Information	The types of documents from where data are collected. They are oral, ephemeral, non-scientific and formal.
Space division switching	A technique in which a dedicated physical path is established inside a switch.
Special	Libraries that collect and store special materials in addition to Libraries others, and serve the specialized requirements of specialist users in anticipation of and in response to specific demands.
Clearing House	An organisation that collects and maintains records of research, development and other activities.
Special Collection	A collection of books connected with local

	history, celebrities, industries etc.
Specifications	A statement containing a detailed description of particulars - as in the terms of a contract or directions on how to make or construct something.
Specificity	Obtaining exact references to query, choosing very specific terms in a search.
Spectrum	A broad range of varied but related ideas, the individual features of which tend to develop so as to form a continuous series of sequence.
Spider	A software program that 'crawls' the web, searching and indexing web pages to create a database that can be easily searched by a search engine
Spider or Crawler	It is a program that automatically fetches web pages for search engines; it is called a spider because it crawls over the web.
Spine	The edge of a book along with the sections are secured together in binding; also called *back.*
Spiral	Winding and advancing like a coil continuously.
Spiral of Scientific Method	A visual path of the research process through its various phases starting from data collection to formulation of theory.
Splice	Editing technique of joining two separate pieces of film together to create a continuous piece.
Split Board	The board used in reinforced library binding, made by two millboards - one thick and the other thin – being glued together, except in the portion to be kept split.
Spreadsheet	It is a big worksheet. This worksheet can be used for data entry and for performing calculations by click of button.
Square	Portion of binding cover that projects beyond leaves.
Staffing	Process of obtaining and keeping the number and type of workers, necessary, to accomplish an organization's objectives.
Standard	A prestige variety of language used within a community.

Standard Cost	A predetermined cost of using some resource (such as labour or materials) in the production of something by the manufacturer.
Standard Deviation	It is the positive square root of the variance.
Standards	Stalidards are rules about the quality or size 01. shape of products, processes, methods, terminologies etc.
Standing Order	i) An order to supply each succeeding issue of a serial or periodical or subsequent volume of a work. ii) An order which is to be acted upon continuously until countermanded.
Standing Vendor	A supplier of books and other reading materials who executes standing orders.
State of an object	The condition in which an object exists. All objects in the universe exist in one of finite or infinite number of states.
Statistic	It is a function of the values of the units that are included in the sample. The basic purpose of a statistic is to estimate some parameter.
Statistical Package	It is software for the collection, organization, interpretation, and presentation of numerical information.
Statistics	It is a broad mathematical discipline which studies ways to collect, summarize and draw conclusions from data. In other words, it is used as a "collection of numerical facts or data".
STM	Science, Technology & Medicine
Storage Device	In computing, a unit into which data can be entered, retained and later retrieved.
Strategy	A strategy is a long term plan of action designed to achieve a particular goal.
Stratified Random	In this sampling procedure the population is divided Sampling into groups called strata.
Stretch and Contraction	Paper, like any other material, has inherent characteristics like flexibility and tensile strength - however small.
Structure	Structurally organized in terms of two levels - level of sounds and level of words.

Structured Observation	It is organized and planned which employs formal procedure. The units to be observed have to be carefully defined.
Style Editing	In particular publications, consistent use of the Mechanics of writing following approved conventions.
Style Manual	A text that guides the editor's decisions on punctuation, use of numbers, abbreviations and other mechanics.
Style Sheet	A style sheet is a set of statements that specify presentation of a document. Style sheets may have three different.
Stylistic	Refers to the level of formality which speakers adopt in
Stylus	Sharp needle tipped with diamond or sapphire used to reproduce sound by setting in the groove of a record as it turns on a record player.
Sub-Committee	A committee that ofthe main committee to work on its behalf hand report to it.
Subject	An organized form of knowledge.
Subject Directory	A search engine service that offers a collection of links to Internet resources.
Subject Gateway	A subject gateway is recognised to be specialized resources on a particular field and is compiled by the people, not robots.
Subject portals	Portals pertaining to specific subjects.
Subject-based	A collection of searchable (and usually browsable) resources Gateway Services descriptions which have been developed by library professionals.
Subschema	A subset or transformation of the logical view of the database schema that is required by a particular user application program.
Subscriber	A user connected to a telecommunication network.
Substantive Editing	Substantial changes advised or made by an editor to improve the language and presentation of a text: make it more interesting

	and easy to read.
Super	A thin, loosely woven, open-meshed, starched cotton fabric used specially for reinforcing books; also called 'mull '.
Surf	Move from website to website on the Internet.
Surrogate	Person or thing that acts or is used instead of another as substitute; an entry standing for a document.
Survey Research	It is a type of descriptive research to study a particular situation, or setting.
Switch	A device that establishes and releases connections between subscribers.
Switched network	A network in which users are connected to a switching system.
Switching	The process of connecting machines, terminals, users, etc. via a Mechanism telecommunications link.
Switching Language	A switching language is one that enables "indexing decisions recorded in one indexing language or classification system.
switching	Transferring information from an inlet to an outlet in a switch.
Synergetic Effect	An effect produced as a result of combination of two or more forces representing more than their mere summation.
Syntactic	Words and their order of representation in a multiword entry of an index file.
Syntactic information	Where informational value of a message is assessed without regard to the meaning of the message.
Syntax	Defines the structure of sentences in a language.
System Analysis	A powerful technique for the analysis of an organization and its functions.
System effectiveness	It is the evaluation of the system performance in terms of degree to which it meets the users' requirements.
System program	Program that helps the computer to perform essential operating tasks and enables the

	application program to run.
Systematic Sampling	In this procedure the units are selected from the population at uniform interval (in time, order or space).
Systems Design	Details how a system will meet the information requirements as determined by the system analyst.
Table of Contents	A table of contents generally lists (and linksto) the most important sections of a document.
Tabular Information	When tables are used to represent logical relationships among data – text, numbers, images, etc.
Tag	A Markup Language encoding feature that describes a discrete component of a document.
Tag 856	A field in UNIMARC and MARC 21 bibliographic format to accommodate electronic location and access related to a bibliographical item.
Takla Makan	Desert occupying the Central part of Sinkiang Province of Western China.
Tanning	The treatment of animal pelts to make leather using vegetables, minerals and animal fats.
Target Readers	Reader for whom a particular writing is meant.
TCP/IP	Stands for Transmission Control Protocol / Internet Protocol, is a suite of protocols that defines the Internet.
Technical	It is the transmission of commercial, industrial, or scientific.
Technical Reports	A report, which provides technical data collated by a committee.
Technological	Expert both internal and external communication star, Gatekeeper having much higher incidence of exposure to the professional literature.
Technological Change	Changes in tools, equipment, processes, actions, materials, and knowledge with which an organisation creates and provides its products or services.

Technological Communication	It is the transmission of commercial and industrial facts and News to the public at large.
Teleconference	A conference with participants in different locations linked by telecommunication devices.
Teletext	A generic term for information services provided by television companies in which data is super imposed on the television signal.
Telnet	It is a program that enables a user to open an interactive login session with a host machine over TCP/IP networks like the Internet.
Term Entry System	A type of post coordinate indexing system in which index entries for a document are made under each of the component terms associated.
Term Relationship	It refers to the relationship between two or more equally concrete things or phrases in a subject.
Term Significance	It refers to the order of significance term in a compound subject heading is the one that is most readily available in the memory of the enquirer.
Terminological	Reference tools that deal primarily with words and phrases, Reference Tools giving meanings or relationships.
Terminology	Standardized terms of any particular discipline.
Tertiary Form of Information	Information generated basing secondary information, sometimes primary information as well.
Tertiary Sources	Sources that are based on secondary sources, or act as key to the primary and secondary sources.
Text	Material that is written or printed.
Theme/topic	Selection of single idea/thought for discussion through Selection testimony, reasoning, emotion, sensory reinforcement, analogy, illustration.
Theory	A coherent group of general propositions used as principles of explanation for a class of phenomena.
Thesaurofacet	Thesaurus which has a classified and

	alphabetical part.
Thesaurus	Book containing lists of words and phrases grouped according to their meaning.
Thesis	Thesis is an idea or theory that is convey as a statement and is explain in a logical way. Thesis is a long piece of writing based on your ideas and research project that part of a university PhD degree.
Third party Software	These are products manufactured or developed by a corporate entity independent from vendor and provided by vendor on a non-exclusive licensing.
Threshold	The minimum level at which a signal of any kind can be detected, either by the human senses or by using any electronic instrumentation.
TIFF	Tag Image File Format (1986) is a common format for exchanging raster (bitmapped) images between application programs.
Time division	A technique in which a shared common resource is used.
Time Study	It determines the time required to perform each element in a job or an operation.
Tissue	Fine quality paper, ideal for repair and restoration work.
TOC	Table of Contents.
Tornadoes	A rotating, funnel-shaped, column of air ranging in width from a few yards to more than a mile and whirling at destructively high speeds.
TQM	Total Quality Management is a modern technique of quality management and quality assurance that takes care of performance.
Trade Catalogue	A publication containing particulars of goods manufactured by, or sold by, a firm frequently illustrated and containing prices.
Trait	Distinguishing feature in character.
Translated Form of Information	Original information is presented in a different language called the target.
Translation	It is a software program designed as an aid for

Memory	human (TM) translators. A translation memory consists of a database of text segments in a source language.
Translucent Screen	A sheet of glass treated in some way (ground, opal, coated, etc.), or plastic, on to which an image is projected in a microfilm reader.
Transmission links	Communication links that interconnect switching systems.
Transparent	In computing, it pertains to a process or procedure involving a user without the later being aware of its existence.
Transponder	A device inside the satellite that receives uplink signals, filters out noise, amplifies and retransmits.
Truncation	A search technique in which a user adds a symbol (such as * or ?) to a word stem in order to retrieve multiple endings of the word.
Turing Test	A test for intelligence in software devised by the British scientist Alan M. Turing.
Typed Message	Agents that interact with each other via typed messages Agents to perform a function.
Typography	The way in which written material is arranged and prepared for printing.
UBC	Universal Bibliographic Control Programme of IFLA.
UBCIM	Universal Bibliographic Control and International MARC Programme of IFLA.
UGC Infonet	An initiative of UGC to provide full-text access to Internationally reputed scholarly journals to the universities in India.
UKOLN	United Kingdom Office for Library and Information Networking.
Ultrafiche	A transparent film of Microfiche size having significantly high number of frames and the original is reduced more than 100 times.
Umbra	Dark central part of the shadow cast by the earth or the moon in an eclipse, referring here to the exact references to a query.
UNESCO	United Nations Educational Scientific and

	Cultural.
UNICODE	Universal code for representing world's scripts in Computers.
Boolean Query	A query that is a Boolean combination of terms. For example, Information AND Retrieval, Vision OR Sight.
Uniform Resource	The syntax for all names/addresses that refer to Identifier (URI) resources on the Web.
Uniform Resource Name	A URI (name and address of an object on the (URN) Internet) that has some assurance of persistence beyond that normally associated with an Internet domain or host name.
UNIMARC	Universal machine-readable catalogue — a standard development under the auspices of a working group set up by IFLA.
Union Catalogue	A catalogue of collections of all the libraries of a library.
Unipolar	Representation of digital signals using voltages of the same polarity.
Unit cost	Cost of producing one unit of a product.
Unitized Microfilm	Roll microfilm cut into small lengths for easy search. Usually unitised microfilms are in strips having 6 frames.
Unshielded Twisted Pair	Unshielded pair of wires that are twisted.
Update	Data manipulation involving adding, modifying or deleting data records to keep data up-to-date.
URI	Uniform Resource Identifier - URIs have been known by many names: WWW addresses, Universal Document Identifiers, Universal Resource Identifiers.
URL	Uniform [universal] resource locator, i.e. the address of a web page. :
CBRI	Central Building Research Institute.
Usability	The value of references retrieved in terms of such factors as their reliability, comprehensibility, currency, etc.
Usage	Use of a language usually not governed by

	grammatical rules.
USB	It is the abbreviation of Universal Serial Bus. USB is a standard port that enables a user to connect external devices.
Use of year	Occasionally software developers prefer to add the year of release to a new version rather than a numeral for their products.
Usenet	Also known as 'news', 'newsgroups', or 'discussion groups'. Usenet is a huge collection of newsgroups about every and any topic one can imagine.
User Agent	Software to access web content, including desktop graphical browsers, text browsers, etc.
Assistive Technologies	Devices used by people with disabilities to access computers. Some assistive technologies.
User effort	It refers to the intellectual as well as physical effort required from the user in obtaining answers to the search requests.
User Group	Synonymous with reader.
User Interface	The contact point or the means by which information is transferred between the user and the computer and vice-versa.
User Orientation	It is study of the process from user ambition to full implementation of new, inhabitable, inspiring, etc.
User Profile	A statement of user's information require ent in specific terms.
ACM	Association of Computing Machinery.
User Profile	Data on any type of readers as a guide for technical writing.
Vacuum Freeze Drying	In this process the frozen records are dried in a vacuum chamber dried at temperatures below 0 C.
Validity	A measure of accuracy of results and their generalization to other situations.
Vapour Phase	An early method for deacidifying books by alkaline gases.
Variable	The quality or quantity of a thing that takes

	different values.
Variable costs	Costs which vary directly wit11 salesfservices value.
Variable Field	A field which can be extended to accommodate longer data as per requirement.
ANSI	American National Standards Institute is an organisation of American industry groups works with the standards committees.
Variance	It is the arithmetic mean of squares of deviations of observations from their arithmetic mean.
Variation	region social class, occupation, sex, etc.
Variety	Standard/languages/dialects/ varieties cut across regional differences, providing a unified means of communication.
Veracity	Truthfulness.
VERONICA	Stands for Very Easy Rodent-Oriented Net-wide Index to Computerized Archives. Developed at the University of Nevada.
Version	A major upgrade in a software product.
Vetting	To submit a text to an expert for examination and improvement.
Videoconferencing	A real time video session between two or more users or between two or more locations.
Videotext	A generic term for system whereby computer based information is made available on an adapted television monitor.
Virtual circuit	A fixed route for information transfer.
Visuals	Information presented in the form of graphics, drawings, photo-graphs, graphs, charts, maps, etc. to complement the printed matter in a text.
Vocabulary control	The technique of using controlled language to describe terms in an information storage and retrieval system.
VPN	A VPN, or Virtual Private Network, is a network that is constructed by using public wires to connect nodes.
VRML	Stands for Virtual Reality Modeling Language.

	VRML is an open, platform- independent file format for 3-D graphics on the web.
VSAT	Very Small Aperture Satellite.
W3C	An international industry consortium which develops common protocols that promote WWW evolution and ensure its interoperability.
WAIS	Stands for Wide Area Information Server, WAIS is a commercial software package that allows indexing of huge quantities of information.
WAN	A computer network that operates across large distances nationwide or worldwide.
Warp	In a piece of fabric there are two sets of thread laid, one across the other, and woven together.
Warping	Bending or twisting or distortion of materials.
Wavelength	The physical distance occupied by one cycle of a signal wave while propagating in free space.
Waxed Paper	Paper impregnated or coated with wax. Used to interleave sheet undergoing wet repair, to prevent them from sticking together.
Web Browser	Software program that allows to access web pages on the Internet.
Web Browsing	Navigating through Internet to reach different websites and accessing their contents.
Web Chat	Web chat is an online tool that enables users to communicate with each other through real-time text messaging.
Web Indexing	Scanning of documents on the websites and creating an index of keywords, etc.
Web Mining	Discovering from websites valuable information that may be hidden in their contents. 3 unite complete.
Web OPAC	The Online Public Access Catalogue which allows users avail the services of the library using internet.
Web Portal	A website that provides general or customized information services.
Web Search Engine	Programs that allow users to search and retrieve information from the web. Search

	Strategies, Processes and Techniques.
Web Server	A web server is either software that manages websites or the hardware on which server software is run.
Web-book	A Web-book is any Website developed so as to publish a concise, discrete amount of information, art, or software.
WebDewey	DDC-22 accessible through the Internet. Amplified Phrase Order : The order of component terms in a phrase achieved by using the necessary prepositions in between them.
Website	A collection of linked HTML pages available via the WWW generally owned or produced by a single institution or individual.
Webzine	A Webzine is any Website constructed so as to publish a concise, discrete amount of information, art, or software on a regular or semi-regular.
Wei T'O	A mass deacidification process using methyl magnesium carbonate to soak books previously vacuum dried.
Weighted Index	Weighted index derives by multiplying the percentage of respondents with the numerical value assign to the scale.
Weighting	A method of the allocation of values to indexing terms by using quantitative figures according to their importance in the document.
Wheat Paste	An adhesive made from cooked wheat flour and water.
Wood Pulp	Wood shredded and used for making paper.
Wild Card	Wildcard Character, in computer science, a keyboard character that can be used to represent one or many characters etc.
Wildcards	Wildcards is a symbol that facilitates search for multiple endings of a word. Wildcards can be used for external truncation or stemming or for internal truncation.
Work Analysis	It is studying the library operations in step-by-step detail.

Work Plan	The plan of your research in terms of the tasks to be done along with the time at which they will be done.
Work Simplification	It is carrying out an activity, step-by-step by breaking it into simple segments. t : Sheet with row
Worksheet Decision Flow Chart	It can be defined as a graphic means of representing work flows.
World Wide	The World Wide Web also called WWW, W3, or just the web is a Web collection of information servers linked.
WORM	An abbreviated form of Write Once and Read Many times. This is also an optical disc.
WOS	Web of Science - of ISI, USA.
Written Document	It is the final form in which a document is produced. It may be a technical article, a short-communication, a conference report, a dissertation, a monograph, a book.
XML	Extensible Markup Language is a subset of Standard Generalized Markup Language (SGML).
XOBIS	An Experimental Schema for Unifying Bibliographic and Authority Records.
Z39.50	A NISO and ISO standard protocol for cross system search and retrieval.
Zenith	Highest point in the spiral of scientific method.